How To
THINK
On Your
FEET

Patrick Quinn

How To
THINK
On Your
FEET

**KOGAN
PAGE**

First published in 1994
Reprinted 1995

Apart from any fair dealing for the purposes of research or private study, or
criticism or review, as permitted under the Copyright, Designs and Patents
Act, 1988, this publication may only be reproduced, stored or transmitted, in
any form or by any means, with the prior permission in writing of the
publishers, or in the case of reprographic reproduction in accordance with
the terms of licences issued by the Copyright Licensing Agency. Enquiries
concerning reproduction outside those terms should be sent to the publishers
at the undermentioned address:

Kogan Page Limited
120 Pentonville Road
London N1 9JN

© Patrick Quinn 1994

British Library Cataloguing in Publication Data

A CIP record for this book is available from the British Library.

ISBN 0-7494-1332-8

Typeset by DP Photosetting, Aylesbury, Bucks
Printed and bound in Great Britain by
Clays Ltd, St Ives plc

For Elaine.
Not only a great feet-thinker,
but also a remarkable lady.

Contents

Foreword

How to Think on Your Feet is a great little book; and so it should be, because the author is very well versed in the subject.

As a copywriter, and in my opinion one of the best you'll find by a long chalk, feet thinking is a daily necessity for Patrick Quinn.

A constant stream of products and services crosses his desk, with their owners' expectations that through his pen sales will flow. And sales are what his clients get, via his unique ability to think laterally and express irresistibly.

You might agree, therefore, that the mind which can extract the most salient property from a host of product features, mould it into a compelling sales proposition, and target the market sector with the optimum potential, is adequately capable of spontaneous retort. Hence, Patrick Quinn is an able teacher of the art of thinking on your feet.

You may be interested to know that he had to learn to think on his feet long before his thirst for literature and words steered him on the course of professional writing. Pat grew up in the East End of London when it was a shade tougher than it is today; and being less than muscular, thinking on his feet was the only protection against playing the role of football on the big guys' team. For him, debate held far more appeal than physical confrontation.

So this book is well authored. It holds the key that will unlock your potential to hold your own. However, it will only work for you if you work for it. The book contains some very smart exercises which, when practised with diligence, will certainly enable you to think on *your* feet.

When Pat sent me the manuscript and asked me to write this Foreword, I saw that Chapter 1 was entitled 'Know thyself'; and it occurred to me that I ought to test this initial precept. So I rang him and asked: 'Do *you* know who you are?'

'Well,' he replied, 'I'm not who I think I am, and I'm not who you think I am. I am, I think, who I think you think I am.'

That's feet thinking for you.

John Powell
Managing Director
The Markethill Group, Bristol

Introduction

'To question a wise man is often the beginning of wisdom.'

German proverb

The gentleman who wrote the Foreword to this book told me a story recently. He said that while on business in Atlanta, he learned of an incident involving the great Fred Herman, who had the reputation of being the world's finest salesman.

Herman was due to speak at a sales convention, and after the organiser had introduced him to the audience, he decided to put Herman to the test. He said:

'So you're the world's finest salesman, Fred?'

'Well, some people are saying so,' Herman replied.

'If that's the case,' said the organiser, producing a glass ashtray from behind his back, 'sell me this ashtray.'

Herman smiled. 'How can I do that? I've been here five hours and I haven't seen you smoke. You don't smoke, do you?'

'No, I don't.'

'Then what earthly good would an ashtray be to you? What could you use an ashtray for if you don't smoke?'

The organiser appeared somewhat disappointed at this reply, but decided to soldier on. 'Um, I could use it for a paperweight, or as a paperclip tray.'

'Yes, but in all honesty, what would an ashtray be worth to you for those purposes?' asked Herman.

The organiser shrugged. 'Well, a dollar at least.'

'All right, then. It's yours for a dollar.'

Verbal salesmanship – the art of converting the sceptical. It has a little to do with thinking on your feet.

Blarney

Back in the 1600s, a chap called Cormac MacCarthymore lived in a castle not far from the port of Cork in Ireland. Now, old Cormac knew a thing or two about shooting a line. He could, so the legend goes, practically charm the birds out of the trees with his silvern tongue and ready wit.

One of these birds was a lady called Elizabeth. That she also happened to be the Queen of England at the time is, I suppose, pretty relevant to the story. Anyway, as time passed, Elizabeth became somewhat circumspect about Mr MacCarthymore's loyalty to herself in particular and to England in general. On a number of occasions she deliberately tested his loyalty and, in almost every respect, found him wanting.

The Queen then despatched her favourite at court, the Earl of Essex, to have a word with Cormac. The gist of the message was: surrender your castle, and renounce your chieftainship in order to prove our trust.

'Certainly,' replied Cormac, and then went on at great and tortuous length about how his allegiance and fidelity was beyond question. The gist of his speech, which was a beautifully structured honeycomb of flattery and blandishment, was quickly conveyed to Elizabeth. She was, for the moment, mollified.

Several months went by but, much to the Queen's fury, it was learned that Cormac was still comfortably ensconced in his castle and was giving no sign whatsoever of leaving.

As we all know, Elizabeth I wasn't the kind of lady with whom you messed, unless you fancied a week or two in the oubliette. She therefore sent a further message, this one reinforced with some pretty dire threats. Back came the reply: 'No problem. I shall be gone in a trice. Just a couple of things of great urgency to take care of first ... blah, blah, blah.'

Finally, after a series of similar exchanges, the Queen became really cross: 'Blarney, Blarney, Blarney! I will hear no more of Blarney Castle or the wretched MacCarthymore!'

Blarney – the art of looking and sounding as though you believe what you are saying. It has just a little to do with thinking on your feet.

Repartee

More recently, it was reported that a middle-aged man held open the door to a department store for a woman of about half his age. The lady in question was not as delighted at this gesture of chivalry as she might have been. In fact, she was miffed. Fixing the fellow with a piercing gaze she said:

'You're only doing this because I'm a woman.'

To which the man replied, 'No, madam, I'm doing it because I'm a gentleman.'

Repartee – the art of the snappy retort. It has something to do with thinking on your feet.

Flannel

Again, a report in *Hansard* just a few days ago shows that a certain Minister of the Crown knew more than enough about turning away wrath; and turning awkward questions to his own advantage.

When asked, at some length, to tell Parliament why his Ministry had done nothing about a particular issue, the Minister replied:

'The honourable gentleman's question has been posed in three parts. In answer to part one, even he must be aware that more money is being spent on — than ever before. In fact, during the previous fiscal year, this government has increased its spending on — by 27 per cent.

'In answer to parts two and three . . . likewise.'

You will notice that he never once mentioned his own ministry, nor acknowledged that it had been in any way tardy nor, indeed, did he attempt to answer the question. Even so, he made a very large point.

In similar vein, a radio interviewer buttonholed a member of the Cabinet with a query about how long a certain project would take.

This is the answer he received:

'Of course, it is always the case in matters of this kind that we cannot predict with any accuracy exactly what the timespan might be for a given undertaking. Especially one as complex as, you must acknowledge, this is. But we are learning the whole time; and we are taking on board what we learn; and we are using these lessons to break what is, after all, new ground.'

Once again, the question remained unanswered.

Flannel. The art of speaking many words without saying anything of any consequence. It has something to do with thinking on your feet.

Misdirection

Politicians are, without doubt, the finest possible examples of 'feet thinkers'. Yet union leaders can easily run them a close second; and the very best of these are beyond parallel.

One of this number was being interviewed on television recently, and the thrust of his argument was his considered opinion of the government's ineptitude insofar as the setting up of a proper railway link with the Channel Tunnel was concerned.

After some preamble, he said: 'It will be ten years before Scotland, Wales and the west of England can reap the benefits of the Channel Tunnel.'

His interviewer nodded briefly, then quietly said: 'Name one.'

The union man blinked, momentarily knocked off his stride. But the interviewer persisted. 'I am asking you to name one benefit of the Channel Tunnel – because some might say that there are no benefits.'

The answer was given without the slightest hint of embarrassment. 'It would take far too long to go into all the benefits of the tunnel. I'm not here to sell tickets for it. But let me say just this. There will be no benefits whatsoever unless this inept government does something about instituting a sound, proper, usable railway link. And not in ten years' time, but now.'

For an even better example of calmness under fire, consider the conversation between a Cabinet Minister and one of the toughest radio interviewers in the business. You should be aware that the politician in question was at one time a serious contender for party leadership and, thus, the job of Premier.

Interviewer: 'I'd like to broaden the question and put this to you. In the light of the fusillade of criticism about the government's apparent lack of leadership, can I ask if you are still, yourself, waiting in the wings as a serious candidate for the leadership of your party?'

Politician: 'Look here – I am a Minister, gainfully employed in trying to promote growth, to promote trade, and to promote jobs. I am enjoying myself and really don't have a moment to think about the kinds of things you are asserting. You may bother yourself with such trivialities but, frankly, I don't have the time.

Of course, should the party as a whole, at some future date, decide that it is time for a new leader, it is not unlikely that I might wish to reconsider my position.

Now, if you want to ask me a serious question I shall be, as always, glad to answer you.'

Interviewer: 'Thank you, Mr —. A pleasure as always.'

Misdirection. The art of saying one thing and meaning something else entirely. It has a little to do with thinking on your feet.

Who this book is for and why

But let's clear a few decks here. This book isn't all about politicians, union leaders, ministerial spokespeople and other such professional 'feet thinkers'. It's about you and me. The ordinary (or even extraordinary) Janet and John who want to be able to communicate slickly, succinctly, authoritatively and even entertainingly straight off the cuff. This book is for people who are going places:

- For people who have a sneaking suspicion that interaction with others is a fast route to the top.
- For people who understand the simple truth that ambition is no substitute for being able to convince those who matter that you have what it takes.
- For people with the nous to realise that it's not what you know, but how you communicate what you know to employers, clients and superiors and audiences alike.

This book is for:

- Salespeople
- Managers
- Educators
- Councillors and counsellors
- Public speakers
- Account executives in PR and advertising
- Spokesmen and spokeswomen.

It's for everyone, in fact, who has to make verbal presentations of any kind whatsoever; and who has to submit to a barrage of questions after the event.

At which point, you might pose the dreaded question: 'Why?' To which I'd reply: 'Because you are the kind of person who wants to do better in your public or private life.'

The kind of person, perhaps, who longs to be able to look a roomful of people straight in the collective eye and bowl them over with your grasp of a given subject. The kind of person, maybe, who knows his or her professional stuff backwards and inside out, but has difficulty putting it across. The kind of person, on the other hand, who can easily present a well-rehearsed, solid, copper-bottomed sales proposition to a client, but who wilts when the awkward, ad-lib questions come bowling over the horizon. The kind of person who aspires to be the life and soul of the party.

Either way, the man or woman who can answer volubly and interestingly has more going for them in the eyes of their peers than those who mumble, who um and ah, and who turn an interesting but immature shade of pink when placed under the spotlight. They also gain more in terms of job satisfaction and salary cheques.

Allow me to put a proposition to you. Human beings communicate, to a greater or lesser degree, by sight, speech, touch and, if you're a believer, telepathy. Given this, I think you'll agree that speech is the most common form of communication. You may also go along with me when I say that it is via questions that we get the measure of others ... and how they evaluate us.

Thus, questions are the cornerstone of this book. Or, rather, the skill of answering those awkward, probing, questions in a believable way is its mainstay.

You may not realise it right now, but there are a dozen different classifications of question. We'll look at these shortly; and we'll examine them carefully. Why? Because, for example, a skilful newspaper journalist can pose questions in such a way that any answer you give will reflect badly, even cataclysmically, upon you, or your reputation, or your company or your family. Or even all four. How do you answer?

A bright job interviewer can ask questions that are cleverly designed to make you contradict yourself. How do you spot these dodges and manoeuvre yourself into a more credible position?

A canny client can present objections that make a complete nonsense of your carefully prepared sales proposition. How do you sweep those objections off the floor?

A tough employer can make your position potentially untenable with black and white facts about declining production output or falling sales figures. How do you inject areas of disarming grey into his arguments?

More to the point, how do you get over these obstacles without indulging in deliberate and calculated lies? After all, lying has a bad habit of coming home to roost and has absolutely no place in our scheme of things. Once people realise that you are prone to the fib, you will never be believed, no matter how honest you are being.

How? I propose to show you right now.

In short, then, this book hopes to achieve three main objectives.

1. To improve your communication techniques.
2. To develop credibility and subject know-how.
3. To improve your relations with others.

And if, along the way, we explore a bundle of related themes, I shouldn't be at all surprised.

One more thing

Oh, just one more thing. What is it, exactly, that makes me some kind of authority on thinking on your feet?

In the first place, as a professional writer of books and advertising copy for around 30 years – along with the odd dalliance with newspapers – I have interviewed any number of celebrities in the artistic, political and literary worlds. What they had to say, and how they said it, remains indelible – if not in my mind, then certainly on paper and on tape.

Similarly, for the purposes of this book, I have talked to behavioural psychologists, public speakers and top salespeople.

Further, as someone who is frequently asked to address audiences on the subject of advertising (probably a case of mistaken identity), I am forced to answer myriad difficult questions on my often unorthodox precepts. So far, I seem to have got away with it.

Finally, I recently did a crash course on speaking off the cuff, where participants were made to talk, for increasingly longer periods, on subjects about which they knew absolutely nothing, and then to defend their propositions under a hail of unfriendly questioning. It was, I can assure you, the most harrowing experience. It taught me a lot.

I hope that a distillation of all of the above will do the same for you.

For the record, in producing this book, I have used the masculine pronoun more often than the feminine. This avoids the problem of having to prefix every he with a she and finishing up with an even more cumbersome read than what you already have. I assure you that no bias exists in my mind; and as for prejudice ... well, quite the reverse.

CHAPTER
1

Know thyself

'There aren't any silly questions, only silly answers.'

Bilbo Smith

T here is a saying that still waters run deep. When applied to people, this piece of homespun Couéism suggests that somehow the quiet ones are the most intellectual. Conversely, it is said, rightly, that empty vessels make the most noise; and there is no doubt that people who like the sound of their own voice can irritate beyond bearing. It might be suggested, however, that the quiet person, the one who sits there and says nothing, is tacitly admitting he has nothing of any importance to say and, by implication, is *thinking* nothing of any importance. Which begs the question: does he have anything to contribute?

Whether this is a correct interpretation is neither here nor there. The fact of the matter is that this is a commonly held view.

We've all been there. Half-a-dozen of us are sitting around a table. The conversation flows back and forth, covering a wide range of subjects. Then someone says, 'What would you do if you won a million on the pools?' Everyone is anxious to answer, except one character, who gulps uncomfortably, shrugs and says, 'Er ... I couldn't really say.' End of conversation.

What this rather simplistic example demonstrates is:

1. Mr Uncertain doesn't have the confidence to help fill a conversation – let alone lead one.
2. He doesn't have the imagination to quickly compile in his head a suitable answer to the question while others are giving theirs.
3. He believes that whatever answer he gives will be derided by his fellows.
4. He plays boringly safe.

Consequently, he lumbers himself with a reputation for being a wet blanket, and the chances are that he won't be invited back. But don't let's pre-judge him. He is probably a thoroughly decent chap. He may care desperately what others think of him. Unfortunately, he refuses to allow the creative juices to flow; the rein he keeps on his feelings is so tight that he can barely walk, never mind gallop.

It's my contention that no matter how introverted certain people may appear, there is inside everyone the ability to rise above it and be creative in their spoken communications. Sure, not all of us can be writers of any reputation; even fewer will be painters and sculptors. But each of us has the power of speech. Meaning the necessary tools to make others sit up and take notice. Real notice.

And it doesn't need a vast vocabulary filled with words nobody has ever heard of. It certainly doesn't require a BBC accent. All it requires is the will ... along with the ability to improvise with ideas.

The very best of jazz musicians, those who can improvise on an original theme and produce a flow of music that is better than the original, are not necessarily better musicians in a technical sense. But the combination of instrumental tone, the phrasing, the ability to build to the climax, puts these people head and shoulders above the rest. They transport their listeners to heights approaching religious fervour. Yet quite a large proportion of them cannot even read music.

What is it that they have which the others don't? They have

the happy knack of being able to unlock and use the whole of their creative mind.

Now for a paradox. Human beings both control and are controlled by their brain. Let me explain. We say to the brain, 'I want to draw a circle'. Without more ado, the brain then tells us to rotate the point of a pencil on a sheet of paper. Result: one drawn circle.

Again, we instruct the brain: 'I have to answer the stupid question about what I would do if I won a million on the pools.' Instantly, the brain tells us how to respond. 'Spend it,' we say cheerily.

How can this be? How can a single element that we call the brain be both master and servant? Well, we could be here all night discussing this and still be no further forward. The favoured theory is that we have, in fact, two brains. One is contained in the left-hand side of that piece of grey sponge, and the other in the right. On the left, we have the logical, plodding, methodical brain. On the right, we have the inventive, creative, 'Have you heard the one about the yellow ferret?' brain.

Now, more often than not, these two biological computers are like neighbours who don't get along too well. They operate pretty much independently of each other: the left brain directing our everyday actions along a fairly narrow path, and the right brain prompting us now and again to change direction, or look up and take stock of our surroundings. And it all works fairly harmoniously. Until, that is, enough adrenalin is pumped into the bloodstream; until enough determination is generated; until we want to do something badly enough. Then they work together with the slickness and confidence of Torville and Dean.

Consider this. You have to make a 15-minute speech to a roomful of strangers. You are nervous at the beginning; you are nervous in the middle; and you are still nervous when you sigh with relief at the end and accept the applause. Now it's question time. The audience wants to quiz you about what you've said. Suddenly, like a damper being opened beneath a fire, a warm glow spreads throughout your body. You are now so relaxed that nothing can break this spell of quiet confidence. And you go on to answer the questions with a slickness and humour that surprises even you.

What has happened is this. In the first place, you controlled that initial nervousness and, instead of running screaming from the room, contained the fear. Such is the flow of adrenalin that you can actually feel its effects as a warm glow once you begin to relax. This warmth makes you relax even further; serenity sweeps over you. You now have the same kind of feeling you experience when you view a beautiful sunset. Everything is just about as right as it can be.

You now have all the conditions to evoke a right-brain response. And, sure enough, up stands right brain and shows you what he's made of.

In essence, you have achieved what some religions call a higher state of consciousness. We all do it from time to time. We win a new job; we get married; we become parents; we qualify for an academic or sporting award. When these wondrous things occur, we are excited to the point where, for a short period, we think ourselves capable of just about anything. At that moment, there is nothing we can't do.

There's the actress who knows instinctively that she has the audience firmly in the palm of her hand. The cricketer who predicts that he is a split-second away from scoring a boundary. The executive who sees that his presentation has convinced the client. These states of mind are, for a happy few, completely involuntary. They just happen. The rest of us have to work at it.

What do we have to do? We have to become excited about our project or subject. We have to get the adrenalin flowing. We have to feel the buzz.

And to reach that higher state of complete confidence when thinking on our feet, the buzz is implemented because we know subconsciously, instinctively, how to improvise with thought and speech.

Which is all well and good if you realise what you are capable of; if you are in contact with yourself; if you *know what you know*.

There's nothing mystical about this. Put simply, the first secret of thinking on your feet is to know yourself. This principle was first mooted by the great Greek philosopher Socrates, and by several thousand imitators since. He said, more or less, that if you don't know yourself, you don't know anything.

The difference between man and animal is that man is aware of his identity. A dog doesn't know it is a dog. A man looks into a mirror and says, 'That is me ... I'. A dog sees its own reflection and observes only a dog. It has no reflective self-consciousness.

The great majority of us spend all our lives trying to deepen our sense of identity. Of course, this is done to a greater or lesser degree, depending on the type of personality we are; but it is particularly noticeable in the young. Teenagers dress in the strangest clothes and act in the weirdest possible ways. These are merely attempts to establish their sense of identity.

Adventure is life's mainstay. People fly aircraft, drive fast cars or go to the Amazon to prospect for gold in order to find excitement; in order to make the adrenalin flow. By facing challenges, and registering how they react to those challenges, they get to know themselves. For the rest of us, those who cannot afford such luxuries or who have other unavoidable commitments, it's vicarious adventure via the exploits of others in books and films. Similarly, we find adventure in the jobs we do and in the reactions to ourselves that we can provoke in others. We find adventure in meeting new people and in making a good impression by way of our actions and conversation. As human beings, we must have it in some shape or form. Life without adventure is a bore.

Why have I gone on about this at length? Simply because no matter what impression you may have of yourself right now, no matter how little (or, indeed, how much) you may think you've achieved, is this impression or sense of achievement an accurate picture? Or is it one thrust upon you by your environment and by other people?

I mention this for good reason. A college tutor once told a certain pupil that he would never amount to much. He turned out to be the genius of his age. In 1935, a respected American engineer commented that the new car developed by a German manufacturer was ugly, noisy, smelly and probably wouldn't sell more than a few hundred models. It went on to become the biggest selling car ever. Again, a noted scientist observed the first experiments with powered flight at Kill Devil Hill and boldly told the waiting press that flying was nothing more than a passing fancy which would never catch on.

Had Albert Einstein, the Volkswagen designers and the Wright Brothers taken any notice of their critics, the world would be a different place. Much different. Just consider for a moment all the brilliant ideas that have never seen the light of day because some expert or other placed the kiss of death upon them.

As someone who has been in the advertising business for practically a lifetime, I can tell you with a certain degree of authority that the great proportion of commercials you see on television, and the ads you see in magazines, are second best concepts or watered down concepts. The truly good stuff rarely gets out of the front door of the agency, for the reason that somebody puts the block on it by 'knowing better'.

What I'm trying to say is that it is *your* concept of yourself which unlocks the buzz, not someone else's. Maybe we should find out exactly what that picture looks like.

Now, you may think that what I am about to ask you to do is a touch puerile and somewhat beneath your dignity. Fair enough. But I would caution you with the observation that quite a number of large international businesses are therefore equally puerile, since they perform a similar exercise upon everybody they recruit – from the tea boy to the marketing manager.

I am asking you to complete the following self knowledge evaluation questionnaire. The purpose is to form a clearer picture of ourselves. A more tangible picture, perhaps, than the one we carry around in our heads.

Complete it, if you will, straight off the top of your head. Write down the first answer that strikes you. Incidentally, there are no right or wrong answers.

Self Knowledge Questionnaire

1. I am a _____ and _____ type of person.

    Choose two of the following to complete the sentence: happy, quiet, kind, jolly, introverted, dissatisfied, romantic, extroverted, sad, colourful, hopeful, ambitious, generous, uncomplicated.

2. Name the man you admire most. _____

3. Which woman do you admire most? _____

4. Your major ambition is _____

    _____

5. Other people see you as _____

6. The best film you ever saw was _____

7. If you were stranded on a desert island, name two people you would want with you.

    _____

8. I think I should have a better job.

    Yes or No? _____

9. My biggest hate is _____

10. The greatest turn-on is _____

11. The one thing I don't like in myself _____

    _____

12. What I dislike in others_____

13. I often daydream about _____

14. If you could be someone else, who would it be? _____

    _____

15. My favourite pastime is_____

16. What car would you like to own? _____

17. I have an   [excellent]   [good]   [average]   vocabulary. Tick one option.

18. What is your favourite sport?_____

19. Imagine you could have any job you wanted – what would it be?

    _____

20. What would you miss most on that desert island? _____

    _____

21. I have the bad habit of _____

22. I need to be liked by others – Yes or No? _____

23. Other people like me because _____

24. I am short-tempered – Yes or No? _____

25. Having completed this questionnaire, I am a lot happier about
    myself. Yes or No? _____

Not as simple as it looks, is it? I imagine you had to think quite carefully about some of the questions; and particularly about those relating to your intimate self, those things that only you know.

If you look back upon what you've written and, if you've been honest (which I don't doubt for a moment), you should be able to learn quite a few new things about yourself. Best of all, by completing the questionnaire, you adopted a positive attitude. You wanted to know yourself. And this is, as Mr Socrates said, the best possible knowledge you could have.

It will, I promise, be of great benefit as we progress.

CHAPTER
2

Questions, questions, questions

'A sudden bold, and unexpected question doth many times surprise a man and lay him open.'

Francis Bacon

L atest estimates put the number of people who speak English at close to one billion worldwide. What's more, English is probably the richest in vocabulary, with half a million words listed in dictionaries. By contrast, German has only about 190,000 words, while French has fewer than 90,000.

It is also true to say that English has more synonyms than other languages. Whereas English might have half-a-dozen words all meaning the same thing, in French there may be only one or two, and in German none at all. To get over this, the German language is stuffed with long, tongue-twisting words which are made up of the conjunction of two, three and even four other words.

Given all of this, it may appear that in terms of vocabulary, the English speaker has a head start when it comes to speaking off the cuff. Yet, if you listen to the best of speakers, you will quickly realise that they use only the simplest of words to make their point. Their vocabulary may be rich in synonyms, but those synonyms are ordinary, everyday words and phrases. Only when they are addressing a specialised audience do they launch into the ostentatious.

To prove the truth of this, listen to a Reith lecturer on the one hand and a literary or drama critic on any of BBC radio's arts programmes. The difference is as night and day. The lecturer attempts to bring the audience under a wide umbrella and make his or her precepts understood by everyone. The art critic seems more concerned with the euphonic structure of his speech than the subject of it. In short, one wishes his talk to be enjoyed and the other wants to enjoy talking.

As far as we are concerned, we shall embrace the former and ignore the latter. Not for us the high-flown phrase built from obscure words. To put it into words of one syllable, we shall put it into words of one syllable.

We established earlier on that questions take up the major part of any verbal communication; and it is by questions that others form their opinions of us. So far, so good.

I propose that we now perform an experiment. Opposite are 12 questions. I'd like you to answer them in numerical order, aloud and off the cuff; meaning without spending time composing your answers. If you can speak into a cassette recorder, or to someone else who is prepared to listen, so much the better. There are only two stipulations: 'yes' or 'no' answers will not do, and each answer must be at least 30 words in length, the equivalent of a full 12 seconds. Try, if you can, to make your answers flow, with no obvious pauses for thought.

The object of this exercise is to gauge your ability to think on your feet at this point. Later on, we'll go through a similar operation. With any luck, you will have improved beyond recognition. There is another reason, but we'll examine that shortly.

One final point. The questions have been chosen so that whatever your present ability, they favour nobody. Were you to be allowed to choose your own topics, you'd obviously select subjects with which you are familiar. Which would be no contest at all. Ready?

1. Have you stopped worrying about what others think of you?
2. What is your greatest achievement to date?
3. Who is the most important person in your life, and why?
4. What single measure could the government introduce to help this country out of the mess it is in?
5. What's the difference between an etymologist and an entomologist?
6. Some might say that you put less than 100 per cent effort into your job. How do you feel about that?
7. The gravy-train is leaving. Will you be on it?
8. Why is your bank account in a false name?
9. Is it true that you disliked all of your school teachers?
10. Is it true that all of your school teachers disliked you?
11. Can you remember the name of your first girlfriend/boy-friend?
12. Your friends are saying that you are getting above yourself with all this reading of self-help books. Are they right?

If you recorded your efforts, play them back and listen carefully to what you had to say. Then ask yourself the following questions. If somebody listened to you, ask them:

1. Did you 'um' and 'ah' during any of the answers?
2. Did you take long pauses as you gathered your thoughts?
3. Did you stumble over words?
4. Did you make extravagant gestures with your hands?
5. Did you play with any object – a pen, your glasses – as you answered?

The newcomer to speaking in public, at an interview, on camera or at the microphone will always commit a few of the above errors; and in some cases, all of them. The 'um' and 'ah' syndrome is endemic to many non-professional speakers; and the problem with it is that it has the listener mentally urging the speaker to get on with it. In its severest forms it can be so annoying as to switch the listener off completely.

Only practice can banish the 'um' and 'ah' from your vocabulary.

This also applies to the long pause and stumbling over words.

The secret of nailing both these hazards is to pace your words at *less* than your normal conversational rate – thereby giving yourself time to think about what will follow; and thereby preventing a shunting of the sentence, where words cannon into each other and produce a stutter.

Which produces our first precept:

ONE: SLOWLY DOES IT

Slow your speech right down to less than normal conversation rate.

You can always increase the pace once fluency has been developed.

What about extravagant hand gestures and fiddling with anything that happens to be lying around?

I am not the greatest public speaker in the country, but over the years, I have spoken to hundreds of audiences. It was not until very recently, however, that it was pointed out to me just what a fidget I am (or, rather, was) on the rostrum. I would spin my glasses in my hand until I had a respectable propeller effect on the go. I would pace up and down in a demented fashion; wave my arms; bang the rostrum; put glasses on and take them off again instantly; and perch half on a desk for a split-second and then get off. The general effect was not conducive to easy listening. And that's the problem. It was pointed out to me by a highly professional trainer that the audience probably cared less about what I was saying than about what contortion I was going to perform next.

I also learned quite a bit about what my body language was saying to these poor, benighted audiences. We'll have a word to say about body language in a later chapter.

TWO: FIDDLING IS FOR VIOLINISTS

Resolve to keep your arms to your sides and your hands off playthings.

Finally:

6. Did you repeat the main theme of each question as a part of your answer?

If you did, you are off to a blinding start as a potential thinker on the feet. Repeating all or part of the question is a splendid way of giving yourself time to collect your thoughts. However, this ploy is less obvious to the listener if you slightly rephrase the question.

Thus, for question 1, you might have kicked off along the lines of: 'You ask me whether I've stopped worrying about what others think of me. That's a good question because...'

Or, for question 2: 'It may be debatable whether I have a greatest achievement; but since you have asked, I shall cast my usual modesty to the wind and say...'

Like this, too, the initial fluency of your reply helps you to dispel any nervousness or self-consciousness you may be feeling. Furthermore, if you attempt the question directly, from cold, as it were, you may find yourself momentarily stuck for a reply. This will result in a pregnant silence, which in turn will result in embarrassment. Clearly, to become proficient at thinking on the feet necessitates the immediate and fluent response to questions. Mental confusion has no place in our scheme of things.

THREE: MAKE THE QUESTION WORK FOR YOU

The artifice of repeating or rephrasing the original question:
  Gains time
  Dispels nervousness
  Prevents awkward pauses.

If, in replaying your answers, you are generally unhappy with the result, or where your listener is not as kind about your efforts as you might hope and they point out your errors with some glee – don't despair. Most people performing this exercise, on the strength of little warning, almost always come across as stilted and uncomfortable.

For that reason, it might be a good idea if you picked just one of the 12 questions and re-did it. And if you can inject a little humour into your answer, so much the better.

For what it's worth, and I assure you that I did not cheat. I answered question 11 thus: 'You ask about my first girlfriend. We were both about 14. Her name was Samantha. It was Sam for short, but not for long. I chased her for weeks. Luckily for her, she escaped.'

The secret of answering questions for which you are unprepared is, I think, to keep the sentences short. Use simple, everyday words.

FOUR: TO PUT IT INTO WORDS OF ONE SYLLABLE, PUT IT INTO WORDS OF ONE SYLLABLE

You can develop your vocabulary once you've perfected the knack of speaking impromptu.

Incidentally, one of the better answers I have been given to question 5 was provided by a lady who is no stranger to public speaking. It ran like this: 'Define an etymologist and an entomologist? All right. While the question seems particularly difficult, the answer is amazingly easy. You see, an etymologist is someone who knows precisely what an entomologist is!'

Being able to think on your feet with such panache as this takes years of practice; and to be able to give the impression that you have all the answers, all the time, requires the dedication of a monk. Oddly enough, the lady in question has not always been a lecturer. In fact, she started off as a common-or-garden secretary in a common-or-garden solicitor's office. As it turned out, though, she discovered a talent for answering 'impossible' questions from the firm's clients. Such was her grasp of the day-to-day affairs of the office that clients preferred to speak to her about the progress of their land purchase or their item of litigation than to the partners. As she points out, every piece of paper that came into or left the office had to pass through her hands, and she took the trouble to read it. Consequently, she had a better overall idea of what was going on than the partners, who dealt exclusively with their own clients and she was therefore able to provide satisfactory answers to any questions levelled at her.

It was only a short mental leap from being the ideal secretary to teaching others how to become the ideal secretary. And from there to lecturing on business management proper. Many of her excellent ideas are employed throughout this book.

And the moral is clear. I see no reason why any of us, having read, marked and learned the principles, should not be able to put ourselves into a position where more responsibility and promotion come as a matter of course. Leastways, we can make our peers sit up and take notice.

CHAPTER
3

And even more questions

'I keep six honest serving-men,
They taught me all I knew.
Their names are What and Why and When,
And How and Where and Who.'

Rudyard Kipling

One of the better answers to an awkward question that I've heard lately came from a grocer who was asked why his prices were higher at weekends. 'They're not,' he responded, 'they're lower during the week.' This underlines the truism that there is always more than one way of looking at things; although it completely fails to explain why it is that if there are two sides to any given question, there is only one answer.

A long while ago, I wrote a column (which happened to be true, as everything I write is) about the time I was accosted by a youth with flashing eyes and floating hair who asked the way to Fort Neaf.

After a lengthy and tedious discussion, it turned out that the place he was heading for was Thornton Heath, which, for the benefit of the provincials among us, is a suburb of London.

What has this got to do with anything? In the first anecdote, we have a straightforward question about prices. In the second, the question is obscured by delivery and lost in translation and might be termed unanswerable. Apart from these, how many kinds of question are there?

When I first began to research it, I was amazed to find, literally, dozens of ways of posing questions. Too many, as it happens, to make any serious attempt at analysing them individually. In the event, I collated them and finally distilled what I am happy to call the Straight Eight Questions. These are:

The straight eight questions

1. The hidden agenda question
2. The multi-element question
3. The hypothetical question
4. The non-variable question
5. The open-ended question
6. The cul-de-sac question
7. The negative question
8. The echo question.

There are, as I've implied, plenty of variations upon these themes; and I am sure to be taken to task by students of query morphology for passing up the opportunity to catalogue the question from A to Z. But let's agree not confuse an already confusing issue, eh? Apart from anything else, I don't think my heart will stand the excitement.

Let's take them in order and try to get to grips with what is implicit in each.

The hidden agenda

This one runs something like this:

Traffic cop: 'I pulled you over, sir, because you seemed to be having trouble with this vehicle. Is it playing you up?'

He doesn't care whether you are having trouble or not. He wants to find out whether your crashing of gears/wobbly steering/use of windscreen washer instead of indicators is a result of unfamiliarity with the car (it may be stolen) or because you are mentally and physically impaired (drunk).

Another version of this is:

Job interviewer: 'If you could begin your career all over again, what changes would you make?'

The object of the question is not to listen to a long list of changes you might wish to make, but to read between the lines and determine whether or not you *enjoy what you are currently doing.*

The multi-element

This is really a series of questions within one question, all designed to lead you along a given answer path.

Barrister: 'The court would like to hear whether you knew that your husband was planning to rob the bank; and if you didn't know, why were you observed by witnesses to be knitting him a balaclava; and why, pray, was an identical balaclava found at the scene of the crime?'

The hypothetical

This one is posed to elicit an out-of-character response and secure an out-of-context quote. It is the stuff of which tabloid newspaper headlines are made. Often.

Journalist: 'If the jury decides against you in your libel action, Miss Starlet, some experts say that you might have to forfeit more than £250,000 in legal fees – how do you feel about that?'

If Miss Starlet answers, as many of us might, that the jury would be less than fair if they found against her, she will be horrified to see the following in the evening papers. JURY UNFAIR SAYS LIBEL CASE ACTRESS.

The non-variable

Meaning non-variable in terms of the desired response. This is similar to the closed question, where only a 'yes' or 'no' answer is expected; but with a slight twist, since the respondent has a fixed choice of answer. Closed questions are rarely asked by professional interviewers. They therefore have no place in our scheme of things.

Salesman: 'You like the product; and you have no worries about the price. Now, when would you like me to deliver – Tuesday or Wednesday?'

The open ended

Open-ended questions are the stock-in-trade of people like personnel officers, journalists and sales people generally. They always kick off with one of six openers: Who, What, When, Where, Why and How; and they are designed to produce the maximum information.

Sales Director: 'Who should take responsibility for researching this new market?' Or 'What makes you think that prospective customers will buy the new service?' Or, again, 'When will be the best time for launching it?'

And so on.

The cul-de-sac

This is another great favourite of television and radio inter-viewers. Its intention is to run the questionee into a brick wall.

Interviewer: 'Minister, the latest employment figures look black for the government. With a 10 per cent rise in unem-ployment throughout the country, I imagine you will now be thinking seriously about your own position in the employment ministry?'

If the minister answers that he isn't thinking seriously about his position, he demonstrates apathy, or a lack of sympathy for the unemployed. If he says he is thinking seriously about his position, the interviewer will then follow up by asking him whether he has discussed his resignation with the prime min-ister. He cannot win – unless he is quick on his feet.

The negative

Should probably be better termed the argumentative question. Its purpose is to put you firmly in your place. 'Are you seriously suggesting that *you* know more about this subject than *they* do?' Or: 'How on earth can you justify a statement like that?'

The negative question puts you on the defensive and is designed to force you to commit yourself to further wild claims.

The echo

Beloved of police officers, this question helps the interrogator to delve ever deeper into the suspect's story. In practice, the interrogator rearranges the suspect's statements into a question; this in turn forces the suspect to re-examine what he has said and enlarge upon it. I have also met some very successful sales people who use the technique to keep the prospect talking and therefore interested.

Interrogator:	'What was on your mind when Brown started trouble with Green in the disco?'
Witness:	'I thought he was crazy.'
Interrogator:	'So you thought he was crazy?'
Witness:	'Yeah – everyone knows what stupid things he does. And I was scared of him.'
Interrogator:	'You were scared of him that night – were you?'
Witness:	'So would you be. He carried a knife; and he had a grudge against Green.'
Interrogator:	'He had a grudge against Green?'
Witness:	'Sure – Green had taken his girl. Brown said he'd kill him.'
Interrogator:	'So Brown was out to kill Green that night?'

Notice how the interrogation begins with an innocuous, seemingly unimportant question, but becomes progressively more serious – and all of the pertinent pieces of information come out of the witness' own mouth. For this reason, he will find it difficult to deny after the event.

Those are the categories as I see them. So from now on, in whatever situation you find yourself, and from whomsoever it comes, you should be able to determine the motivation behind the question simply by identifying the type of question being asked. Because we now know that the object of questioning is both to elicit and manipulate information.

Before we go on to discover how to respond in the best possible way to the various types of question, I think some pointers on your own attitude under interrogation might be in order.

Lie signs

The British police force, and certain sections of the armed forces, now look upon the interrogation of suspects as a very scientific business. Whereas in past years police officers picked up their interrogation techniques on the job, from working with and watching more experienced colleagues, many now undergo stringent training courses. The object, obviously, is to get the best possible result, in the shortest possible time, without infringing the legal rights of the prisoner concerned.

More or less the same applies to personnel officers and those in business, whose job it is to pick the most suitable candidate for the job at the lowest possible cost in time and money.

It is also no secret that the average clinical psychologist is trained to aim questions at patients and evaluate not only the verbal answer but also the concomitant physical response.

It goes without saying, too, that the best of salespeople are instinctive in their use of interrogative techniques.

In all of these cases, the interviewer will be trying to force the interviewee to go that extra mile in terms of reaction. The police search for a crack in a prisoner's story and attempt to prize it open. The personnel officer probes the potential employee's experience and demeanour in order to assess suitability. The psychologist delves into the reasons behind the answers he receives and searches for sign of trauma. And the salesman establishes his customer's needs so that he can sell the benefits of his product. Oddly enough, each of them looks for the same verbal and non-verbal clues in the interview.

They look for buy signs and lie signs.

Since this is not a book about selling, but is a book about selling yourself, we can safely ignore the buy signs and go baldheaded for the lie signs. This doesn't suppose for a moment that you will be contemplating lying as a matter of principle. The problem with lying is that you will almost certainly be found out; and once found out, will never be believed again. There are times, however, when for reasons of political and business policy, for self preservation or the protection of others, you will need to hedge a little or exaggerate somewhat. Similarly, if you are suddenly projected into a question and answer situation for which you have been allowed no preparation time, you will be understandably nervous. At times like these, the mouth is saying one thing, while the body may say something else entirely – giving the game away completely. In such circumstances, you must be able to recognise whether your brain and body are in total harmony.

Below are the classic lie or nervousness signs. They can be physiological manifestations, or they can be evident in displacement activity. Just as the conjuror distracts the eye from his trickery, so the nervous person performs overt and often exaggerated activity.

NERVOUS IS AS NERVOUS DOES

Trembling	Talkative
Lip licking	Fidgety
Fast blink-rate	Foot tapping
Stammering	Finger drumming
Nervous laugh	Lip biting
Nervous cough	Fingernail biting
Voice pitch rises	Head touching
Yawning	Picking lint from clothes
Sweating	Ear lobe pulling
Increased heart rate	Excessive smoking
Sighing	Closing eyes for long periods

As we've said, the trained interviewer can read these signs as second nature. It's also worth noting that the average audience will pick up on many of them purely by instinct.

Good enough reason, perhaps, to adopt the relaxation exercises and get to grips with the body language messages outlined in later chapters.

But we are, or should be, talking about your attitude to questions here. So I'd now like to lay half-a-dozen rules, based on what we've already discussed, for determining your attitude and frame of mind when called upon to answer up.

Six vital rules of conduct

1. Always look directly at the questioner. Make frequent eye-contact, but don't stare him out. If you have to look elsewhere momentarily, move the entire head, not the eyes alone. Excessive eye movement gives you a shifty air.
2. Adopt an expression of intelligent interest and concern for the subject. An occasional nod demonstrates that you are in control of the situation. Likewise, it can often cause the interviewer to lose the thread of his argument somewhat and, thus, force him to present a less controversial question.
3. Listen carefully to the question; and listen for the issues behind the question.
4. While listening, never attempt to pre-judge the hidden issue, or frame the answer before the questioner finishes. Hold your enthusiasm to answer in check; because if you start to answer the question that you *think* is being asked, and it turns out to be something else entirely, you will be swiftly interrupted, corrected and, no doubt, highly embarrassed. You lose credibility.
5. Once you have understood the question, but need time to compose an answer, play it back by repeating it or, better, by rephrasing it. Rephrasing also helps you to counteract any hostility which may be underlining the question, since you will choose your words carefully – and these words will be considerably softer than the originals.

6. The most innocent-sounding questions often have a hidden motivator – especially in a selling situation. To draw out the hidden interest behind the question, provide a brief answer, then counter with something like: 'Why do you ask?' or 'I'm interested in why you should ask.' This is usually effective in drawing the prospect out, and allows you to provide a more detailed answer or a solution to a problem.

Fear of failure

Even the cleverest of feet thinkers now and again come off second best. It's inevitable. The more you stick your chin out, the more opportunities you give to others to take a sock at it. A very old pal of mine, commenting recently on the definition of failure said: 'Failure isn't about stumbling and falling down. Failure is about stumbling and falling and *staying* down.'

There are any number of well-meaning courses and seminars on the kind of subjects we are covering here. Things like public speaking, surviving job interviews, making better business presentations, personality grooming, and ways of handling press and television buttonholers. Almost without exception, they boast in their literature that their method is foolproof.

Techniques which suggest they can forecast in advance the success of their students, I view with deep suspicion; and the subsequent fees for such courses I contemplate with humour, but also envy. The possible permutations of any given feet-thinking situation are as numerous as the stars in the heavens. Within very broad parameters, techniques such as these can indicate whether or not you are up to it. Within very broad parameters, techniques such as these can demonstrate what can be achieved and how it can be achieved. What they cannot tell you – ever, in a million years – is whether the situations you propose to put yourself in will end up as resounding successes every single time.

So, if I haven't said it already, I'd better tell you that the precepts laid down in this book will only work if you, in turn, work at them. You must adopt and adapt. You should mould these ideas around your own personality. What's more ... you must remember that you can't win 'em all.

Another friend of mine, who also happens to be a comparative psychologist, was quite adamant when she suggested that fear of failure very often prevents us from finding out who we really are. She tells me that recent research shows how something like half of the working population dislike, or actually hate, their jobs. Remarkably, however, only a small proportion of them have any plans for changing occupation.

Apparently, they would rather play desperately and dully safe than take the risk of changing from something they dislike, but have come to depend on, to something which might arguably be better, but which is a strange and unknown quantity.

The problem with playing desperately and dully safe is that you end up with a desperate and dull life. But, according to my psychologist friend, things are far worse than that.

She maintains that playing it safe often means going along with the expectations of others. We do so, perhaps, on the grounds that should it all go wrong, we can always put the blame on them. So, by doing what is expected of us, we are protecting ourselves against failure. And if we're unhappy it is, of course, their fault.

Fear of failure makes us take jobs and adopt roles that we don't like and which are not us.

After a while, we start to behave according to the moulds that others have poured for us. We refuse to take risks; and we decline to stand on our own two feet and go public with something a little out of the ordinary, on the grounds that, as sure as eggs are eggs, someone is bound to disagree with it.

Well, certainly they will.

As we've started to find out. That's whole point of it. And that's the fun of it!

CHAPTER
4

Say it like it is

'Questions show the mind's range, and answers its subtlety.'

Joseph Joubert

In the last chapter, we defined the eight question categories
and roughly outlined their relative differences. What we
ought to do now is examine precisely how these different
types of question may be answered.

But first, a word to the wise. When people ask a question of
you, they do so for one of three specific reasons.

1. They want information which they don't already have.
2. They're looking to confirm something they already know.
3. They are probing to find out more about you.

There are, I'm sure, a whole list of subtle variations on these
themes, but these are enough to be getting on with.

Something else, too. The length and depth of any response
usually depends on the type of personality making the
response. The extrovert, for example, will not only answer the
immediate question, but will then go on to cover an entire
geographia of peripheral areas. This is not an answer, it's a
speech. If they had wanted this character to make a speech,
they would have had tickets printed.

The introvert, on the other hand, responds with the minimum

of information. It may be factual, but it has no life or sparkle. Which reminds me of the parachutist who landed in a tree. Having no idea where he was, he hailed a passing yokel. 'Where am I,' he asked. 'You're up a tree, mate,' replied the yokel. This answer may have been completely accurate, but it told the questioner nothing he didn't already know.

I am sorely tempted to examine at some length the myriad types who fall between these two character groups, especially that well-known chap we sometimes accost at the roadside for directions. He goes on at great and tedious length to tell us how to get from A to B and, because he has formed the impression that we are not particularly bright and may not be able to grasp the issue at first telling (well, we *are* lost), he then repeats the entire set of instructions over again.

Where, then, is the happy medium? What comprises the perfect answer? According to people I've spoken to who earn their livings by posing questions, the best possible answer is made up of two elements.

The components of the perfect answer

1. A concise opening declaration which answers the given question.
2. A supporting statement that reinforces the initial comment eg a statistic, a quotation from a well-known authority, or a well-considered opinion.

This two-pronged approach allows an informative, authoritative, well-rounded reply. It leaves nobody in any doubt that you are a master of your subject; and you sound like just the sort of person that they would wish to do business with.

FIVE: ALWAYS PROVIDE AN ITEM OF SUPPORTING INFORMATION

Turning the features of a product into benefits is the oldest trick in the advertising book. Backing your ideas and statements with supporting facts and figures performs the same job and is the best way, by far, to convince a questioner.

Anyway, let's provide some suitable answers to our question categories.

Hidden agenda

Job interviewer:
'Are you aware that if you are offered this post, you will be responsible for our largest department, and you will receive the fourth highest salary in the company?'

The interviewer knows that you are overjoyed at the prospect. Otherwise, why would you be there?

The object of the question is not to gauge your enthusiasm, but to determine whether you are motivated by power, or by money – or both. All companies are different; and so are the criteria by which they hire staff. Some dislike the power-hungry on the grounds that such people tend to build disruptive empires. Others won't take on the money-mad, since people of this kind may employ unethical practices in order to make extra profits for the company and larger salaries for themselves. I'm not saying they're right or wrong, just that it happens to be so.

Thus, any answer to this question, while covering all the relevant points, must be designed to disarm. Something along these lines perhaps.

Answer:
'I am certain that I can handle the responsibility of running one of your most important departments. My CV shows that I have been working towards just such responsibility throughout my entire career. You will also see that in enlarging my experience, my value to the respective companies has been reflected in my salary.'

With this answer, the interviewee is saying, first, that he has a career plan in which running a major department is a natural progression and, second, that he gets paid what he's worth.

The multi-element

The problem with answering questions of this kind is that you have to remember each of the elements. If you don't, you will quite often be owning up to things you haven't been accused of.

Local radio DJ:
'Thanks for coming into the studio, Mr Grimshawe. Now, as you know it has been widely alleged that your company is guilty of discharging noxious substances into the River Bung, thereby causing widespread pollution and environmental damage. So tell me: is there some process for monitoring outflows from your plant; and if so how rigorously do you apply that monitoring; and why, in this case, has it failed so miserably?'

The secret here is not to rise to the bait and admit to the charge.

Answer:
'I'm glad you used the word alleged when referring to my company, because there is no proof whatsoever that our plant was responsible. And I have to tell you that we've set up an internal inquiry which will investigate the matter fully.

But allow me to answer your question properly. We certainly do have machinery for monitoring outfall into the river. This system is approved by the Rivers Authority and we take it extremely seriously. Of course, systems operated by human beings cannot be foolproof; and if the enquiry shows that the system broke down on this occasion, we shall take every step to rectify it.'

An addendum might be bolted on at this juncture, the thrust of which is to point out to the listeners that your company butters some of their bread.

'My company has operated within this community for 20 years. We employ 450 people from the community. And it is in everyone's interests that the matter be resolved immediately...'

Nice one, Cyril.

The hypothetical

This is a form of questioning beloved of television and radio journalists. Its purpose is to take the person being questioned well beyond their notional standpoint: to force him or her to speculate and, therefore, make statements which, at some later date, may be thrown back into their face.

The interview usually runs like this:

Journalist:	'Jane Grahame, can you explain why, in the light of last week's horrific crash on Tyneside, your company has decided not to ground all 757 aircraft?'
Jane Grahame:	'Yes, I can. We feel that until the Civil Aviation Authority's investigation reveals the true cause of this dreadful accident, we will achieve nothing by grounding aircraft.'
Journalist:	'So, despite the fact that 120 people have lost their lives, your company, British Aviation, will continue to operate 757s until the CAA tells you otherwise?'
Jane Grahame:	'At the moment, the cause of the accident is unknown and there is no evidence to suggest that there was any operational problem with the aircraft.'
Journalist:	'Nonetheless, you are asking passengers to take your word for it and, perhaps, put their lives at very grave risk?'
Jane Grahame:	'The maintenance procedures and air-worthiness of all aircraft in the UK are monitored by the CAA. I can tell you that our own procedures are carried out to the letter. Passengers should be assured that if we had even the smallest doubt about our aircraft, immediate action would be taken.'

Here it comes:

Journalist:	'Let's suppose – just suppose – that a 757 from your fleet falls out of the sky tomorrow, at whatever cost to human life – won't that make a terrible nonsense of your decision to continue operating the aircraft?'

Jane Grahame:	'Whenever an accident occurs to an aircraft, a full and thorough investigation is launched as a matter of course. We are cooperating fully with the current investigation. As I said earlier, until such time as the cause is proved, there is little to be gained from grounding aircraft.'
Journalist:	'But what if it did happen again? What then?'
Jane Grahame:	'I think no reasonable person would expect me to speculate on such a circumstance. The best course is to await the result of the investigation.'
Journalist:	'Jane Grahame – thank you.'

This example goes on a little but it is, as a matter of fact, a close representation of a television interview conducted a year or two ago. It is, therefore, well worth including.

Notice how Jane Grahame stuck rigidly to her guns and refused to be drawn. The average untrained person would, I'm sure, have indulged the interviewer and provided the conjecture he was hoping for; perhaps finally acknowledging, however tacitly, that her company was in error for allowing aircraft to continue operations. As ordinary viewers, ill-informed about aviation matters, we could easily be tempted to back the interviewer's line of argument on the substance of an unwisely answered hypothetical question.

The secret, when answering hypothetical questions, is to do no more than rephrase and reiterate your previously well-defined statement.

You will know that the 'what if' game is played far and wide throughout the land. 'What if you don't pull this account?', 'What if they don't like our prices?', 'What if the sky should fall on his head?' 'What iffers' are trap-layers; they watch to see which path you are treading, then they lay the snare right across it.

Here's a conversation I overheard in an advertising agency not a week ago:

   Mr A: 'We've only two days to prepare this marketing report.'
   Mr B: 'We can do it.'
   Mr A: 'But what if we don't get all the figures?'
   Mr B: 'Don't panic, they're coming.'
   Mr A: 'S'pose they don't?'
   Mr B: 'I'll cut my wrists.'
   Mr A: 'Oh, come on, Ian – that's not the attitude.'

Amazing isn't it?

The non-variable

Imagine you are attending a company management meeting. Present are the heads of the various departments, including yourself, along with your managing director. It transpires that a large client organisation has taken its business elsewhere, which means that a cut in overheads is imperative. Thus, the purpose is to determine where and how staff reductions can be made as a matter of urgency.

Now, everyone present wants to maintain the status quo; not only because they do not relish the invidious task of firing people with whom they may have worked for years, but also because a slimming down may trigger lower output or reduce sales figures. All of which will reflect badly upon the managers concerned.

Each of the managers is told, in turn, that they must lose three people from their respective departments; and the names of the dear, nearly-departed are decided upon there and then. Then the MD fastens his eye upon you for the first time.

   He says: 'You've never really worked by the book – have you, Mike? Don't get me wrong, I admire your one-man sales crusade. Everyone says you are a dynamo; and, to be honest, it seems to work. On those grounds, I reckon you could lose four, maybe five, from your department and never know the difference. Just name the five.'
   You: 'I accept your praise, JB; and I'm glad you

appreciate what I do. But it happens to be a fact that, without all my people putting their heads down, processing the orders, writing the specs and getting the estimates out, I wouldn't have time to do what you acknowledge I do best. They provide the back-up I need; and even then they're hard-pressed to do it. So, if I were to lose just one of them, you'd quickly see a difference. What do you really want – greatly reduced profits or a slightly decreased overhead?'

Such a response should have the effect of defusing a bad situation. You will have noticed that, in replying, you first gave back the gist of the faint praise awarded to you, but you gave it back in a much more polished shape. Second, you made a case for retaining staff which did not depend upon your reluctance to fire them, which the MD would have instantly overruled. Third, you threw the entire proposition straight back into his lap with a non-variable question of your own.

The open ended

As we discussed in the previous chapter, open-ended questions always kick off with: Who, What, When, Where, Why and How.

If we use any of these in the context of the previous scenario, it is clear that far more informative, if less sensational, answers can be received. For example:

Journalist:
   'Who took the decision to keep your 757s flying?'
   'When will you have the results of the inquiry?'
   'How can you justify not grounding aircraft?'
   'Why will you not ground aircraft when, patently, so many lives are at risk?'

This shows us quite clearly that the open-ended question is an extremely dangerous tool in the hands of the skilled interrogator; and it is difficult for the spokesperson to avoid giving a straight answer.

By far the best way to deal with it is to divide the response into two parts. The first part being a straightforward statement of fact; and the second part a qualification, or amelioration, of that fact. Like this:

Journalist: 'Who took the decision to keep your 757s flying?'

Spokesman: (Part one) 'The decision was taken by management in consultation with engineering staff, and with Civil Aviation Authority officials.'
(Part two) 'Obviously, should the picture change as the investigation progresses, then we will reconsider the position.'

Or, perhaps, like this.

Journalist: 'Why will you not ground aircraft when, patently, so many lives are at risk?'

Spokesman: (Part one) 'This is the easiest of all your challenges to rebuff. As a responsible airline, operating routes worldwide, passenger safety is our prime concern.'
(Part two) 'Our decision not to ground aircraft was taken only after we were certain that safety would not be compromised.'

As an aside, here, no spokesperson worth their salt would offer any hard and fast guarantees eg 'We'll never pollute the river again,' or 'My staff are so valuable that I shall never sack a single one of them.' Or 'None of our aircraft will ever crash.' Such warrants tempt fate; and sure as fate, the very next morning the river will be a lovely shade of yellow.

The cul-de-sac

Barrister: 'The plaintiff has told the court that you used obscene language and were aggressive towards her. Wouldn't you agree that aggression and obscenity are greatly to be deplored when employed by a male against a female?'

Oh dear. Whatever direct reply you make to this suggestion is calculated to turn the sympathies of the court away from you. If you say: 'Yes, I do,' then the court naturally assumes that you are tacitly admitting to the charge in the first part of the question. And, clearly, you can't say: 'No, I don't.'

Often, too, in a situation like this, the interrogator will insist on receiving only a Yes or No answer. But we'll get to that in a minute.

How can you acquit yourself? Your answer must go along these lines:

'I was brought up to believe that men should never behave badly towards women – whatever the provocation. What's more, I've practised this principle all my life. Therefore, the lady's complaint against me is at best imaginative, and at worst untrue.'

However, I have to say that if you are guilty and employ such an answer to get yourself acquitted, then you are, sir, a cad of the first water.

So what about the barrister's insistence on a simple Yes or No? The plea in this instance has been given to me by a serving police officer who has much court experience. 'Sir, this court has been assembled in order to assess *all* the facts of the case. I would respectfully suggest that, with a simple yes or no answer, the court would be deprived of the opportunity to hear the true depth of my evidence and therefore unable to reach a wholly accurate conclusion.'

He says it works. He also related a very interesting incident which happened to him in a courtroom; which has a good deal of relevance to this book; which demonstrates that interrogators don't always have the best cards; and which I'm sure you won't mind hearing.

Let's set the scene. It's fairly common knowledge that the prosecution advocate in a criminal law case is not allowed to tell the jury about any previous convictions logged against the defendant. This is a praiseworthy rule, since it negates prejudice building up in the minds of the jury. After all, it is easy to assume that if the man in the dock has committed a similar offence in the past, there is a likelihood that he is guilty of the one with which he is presently charged.

Also, it is fairly universally known that there is little love lost between defence counsel and police witnesses. This is understandable on the grounds that the barrister is being paid vast sums to demonstrate that the police evidence is arrant nonsense, and that his client is as innocent as the day is long.

Therefore, advocates will employ any legal technicality, however finely drawn, to bring the case to a satisfactory end.

You may be aware, too, that witnesses who have appeared in a criminal prosecution are not allowed to talk about the case to other witnesses who have still to go before the court. The reason, obviously, is to prevent stories being concocted in the light of what has already gone on in the court.

All right. The case in question concerned a matter of aggravated assault; and the police were fairly certain that the prisoner at the bar was the culprit. He had a long list of previous convictions for similar offences, and he was, by common consent, a double-dyed villain.

Anyway, the case proceeded and two police officers were called to give evidence. The court then broke for lunch. During the lunch break, the two police witnesses were spotted by a member of the defence team actually drinking in a pub with two other officers – both of whom were due to give evidence in the afternoon session. It was fairly clear, too, that the four were talking about the accused.

When the court reassembled, the barrister quickly called one of the police officers into the witness box. With a wicked smile he said: 'I suggest to you, sergeant, that you spent the lunch-hour with officers who had already given evidence against my client to this court. Is this true? Just answer yes or no.'

'Yes, sir,' replied the sergeant.

'Am I correct in thinking that you discussed my client with these officers? Just answer yes or no.'

'Yes, sir,'

'You stand there and admit that? Just answer yes or no.'

'Yes, sir.'

'Then will you please – in your own words – inform the court about what was said?'

The sergeant hesitated.

'Well?' pressed the advocate.

'I would rather not say.'

The barrister's face turned white. 'But I insist, Sergeant. Please tell the court what was discussed with those officers.'

'I don't think it would be in the interests of the court, sir,' replied the sergeant.

'Oh, really?' Turning to the judge, the barrister said, 'M'Lord, will you please direct the witness to answer my question?'

Nodding tight-lipped agreement, the judge informed the sergeant that he had no choice in the matter.

Then the advocate prepared to deliver the coup-de-grace. 'Now, Sergeant,' he began, 'tell the court exactly – *exactly* mind – what was said.'

'Well, sir,' the sergeant replied stone-faced, 'we were talking about your client's 15 previous convictions for car-theft, breaking and entering and ... aggravated assault.'

The negative

Your company has announced half-year profits of £10 million; yet it is about to lay off 400 workers. The reason for this, as you well know, is that the installation of modern technology has rendered many of the workforce redundant. Also, your shareholders expect a large return on such an excellent profit base. What's more, to stay competitive in a highly competitive market, you have to pare overheads to the bone.

Which is all well and good until the local television station latches on to the news of your plans. And you are the one chosen to represent the company.

TV anchor woman: 'Yours is a very successful company, with a £10 million declared profit; yet you are laying off 400 of the workforce. Is this really the way for responsible people to behave during an economic recession?'

Or, maybe:

TV anchor woman: 'This country needs employment more

than anything else. But if companies lay off workers in such a shoddy manner as you are proposing, where are the new jobs coming from?'

If you were to answer either of these questions in the same tone as they were asked, you would sound appallingly uncaring and smug.

The best bet is not to react to the question itself, but to make a simple statement about new technology, and market competitiveness, as outlined at the beginning. Better still, you should make it very clear that your company's actions actually *guarantee* the working future of staff who are not being fired. After all, if you employ staff to stand around doing nothing, the whole thing will collapse like a house of cards and nobody will have a job. This will turn the negative question into a positive answer.

Certainly, you should never stand on your dignity and defend your case with the proposition that the only reason companies are in business is to make profits – and that includes you; because such an idea is, in the eyes of the general public, so emotive as to be practically indefensible. Over-reaction to a negative question never pays. Just consider the number of TV interviews you've seen in which the subjects have lost their tempers. They gave the impression that their huff had arrived and they were getting ready to leave in it. Were you sympathetic at the time? I shouldn't think so. Are you sympathetic now? Probably not.

Petulance and overt displays of hurt feelings are some of the less admirable traits of the human being.

The echo

Company buyer:	'When we spoke last week, you promised delivery at 9 am this Monday. Today is Tuesday and the units we ordered from you haven't arrived. Why?'
Saleswoman:	'Mr Grief, I do apologise for the delay; but it's due to events beyond my control?'
Company buyer:	'Beyond your control?'

Saleswoman:	'I'm afraid we've had trouble with our assembly line.'
Company buyer:	'Oh, you've had assembly-line trouble?'
Saleswoman:	'Indeed. The main computer has crashed; though we've technicians working on it right now.'
Company buyer:	'Your technicians are working on it?'
Saleswoman:	'Yes – and we should be on-line again by Thursday.'
Company buyer:	'You'll be on-line by Thursday?'
Saleswoman:	'This means your order will be processed by Friday. And I shall personally be at your office at nine to oversee installation.'
Company buyer:	Frankly, I can't wait that long. You may take it that the order is cancelled.'

What went wrong? The saleswoman was being perfectly honest. Well, that was what went wrong: she told her customer too much. And since she must have known that he was an echo questioner, she ought to have been ready for him.

Let's try again.

Company buyer:	'When we spoke last week, you promised delivery at 9 am this Monday. Today is Tuesday and the units we ordered from you haven't arrived. Why?'
Saleswoman:	'Mr Grief, I do apologise for the delay. I can, however, definitely promise delivery to you by Friday.'
Company buyer:	'You promise delivery by Friday?'
Saleswoman:	Yes. I will personally be at your office at nine to oversee installation; and to make sure that you are satisfied. I hope you'll be happy with that?'

He'd have to be churlish to turn her down. And you'll notice that by ending on a question, she left no room for further echo. This is the only way to muffle little sir.

I said earlier that in order to gain time before you produce your answer, you might care to ask to have the question repeated. Fine. But what if your questioner is belligerent and impatient; and won't brook any prevarication?

You can, more often than not, find yourself in such a situation at a job interview, at which time, asking for repetition or clarification of questions is easily seen by a professional interviewer for what it is. What's the solution? Maybe we should play it out here and now.

Interviewer: 'We are an aggressive company. We sell and we sell hard; and we are often accused of being unethical in our techniques. I'd be interested to hear your views on this.'

Hold your horses – don't rush into a reply. You know exactly what he means: the firm probably gives substantial free gifts to company buyers as an incentive for taking their product, or buys inside information about their competitor's projects.

You: 'First, I think I'd have to ask you to give me your definition of unethical in this context.'

Interviewer: 'Well, we don't break the law; but we sail pretty close to the wind.'

You: 'In that case, just so long as I won't be expected to act unlawfully, I'm all in favour of any strategy that gets sales and makes profits.'

In asking to have a word or phrase defined, you will practically force the interviewer to answer his own question.

'Could you explain how you see "marketing philosophy" in this context?'

'Would you give me your definition of "value added" as you see it?'

'I'd like to know how you define "quality time" before I can give you an answer?'

All of these examples are designed to give you a better handle on the question. Use this ploy with impunity.

SIX: QUESTIONING IS A ONE-SIDED CONTRACT

It's worth remembering that when you volunteer to answer a question, you are entering into a contract. And there are no get-out clauses.

While I know there must be at least half-a-million variations on the themes I've outlined in this chapter, I hope it has shown that no question is so difficult that it cannot be answered informatively and in such a way that your credibility never comes into the frame.

Before we close this chapter, just one further thought. Or, rather, four further guidelines that must be in your mind before you even attempt to open your mouth:

1. Listen carefully to what is being asked. Don't ever jump the gun and interrupt on the assumption that what is being asked is what you *think* is being asked.

   For what it's worth, whenever I'm moving into the question and answer session after a seminar, I recite to myself that well-known verse by Hughes Mearns:

   > As I was going up the stair,
   > I met a man who wasn't there.
   > He wasn't there again today,
   > I wish, I wish he'd stay away.

   This has the effect of forcing me to pay strict attention to what is being asked and not to see men on stairs who aren't there.
2. Relax.
3. Organise your thoughts and start framing the reply as the question progresses.
4. Put your brain into gear before operating mouth.

Finally, the first phrase of an answer is always the most difficult to deliver, prone as it is to 'ums' and 'aahs' and the tongue glued immovably to the roof of the mouth. There is a neat method for ensuring that the opening, at least, is intelligible. We'll come to that in a moment.

CHAPTER
5

Be a better speaker

'The voice is a second face.'

Gerard Bauer

When you're feeling happy, the happiness is reflected in your voice. People don't have to see you to know that you are on a high. This is borne out graphically by the training methods of the telephone salespeople. 'Put a smile into your voice by actually smiling as you speak,' they say. And it works.

The converse is also true. When you're unhappy, your voice makes your state of mind very clear; and this applies to anger, nervousness and fear, also. As Mr Bauer (above) so succinctly put it, the voice is a second face.

It will therefore pay you dividends to realise that a bright demeanour produces a happy and confident voice. It's really a matter of luring the left brain into a sense of false merriment by telling yourself: 'I may be scared witless at the prospect of facing this interviewer/audience/microphone, my palms may be sweating and the shirt stuck to my back but, by the Lord Harry, they've got to admire my nerve!'

SEVEN: SMILE AND YOUR VOICE SMILES WITH YOU

I once saw the inimitable Sammy Davis Jr, on stage, performing some intricate juggling manoeuvres with a pair of Colt .45 revolvers. Being one of the world's great song-and-dance men, gun-play was not something to be expected of him. Anyway, halfway through the routine, he stopped, looked the audience straight in the collective eye and said: 'Don't panic. I wouldn't do it if I wasn't good at it.'

In retrospect, I am absolutely convinced that his outward calm was an act. Inside, he was as nervous as anyone can get. His words, I think, were testament to it.

Similarly, and for what it's worth, people in a position to know the truth of it say that the late Sir Laurence Olivier was often so overcome with nerves before making a stage entrance that he would be physically sick. Did any of his thousands of audiences ever know, for one second, just how badly he was suffering? Absolutely not.

Olivier knew the many-splendoured fact that once he had delivered his initial lines, once he had got into his stride, there was nobody on earth to touch him.

So why cannot we take a leaf out of this book? Surely, when we make our next entrance at that job interview or on that TV programme, we can just as easily put on a brave front and a bold face, and nobody will be any the wiser? Not if we have the facts, the figures and the whys and wherefores of our particular forte at our fingertips, they won't.

Well, this is only half the story. The next element in our feet-thinking equation is fluency.

Fluency

There are those among us who can speak at length about nothing in particular. Having only a cursory understanding of a particular topic should not prevent you from pontificating about it at great length. Ask any politician. Thus, ignorance of a subject should be no bar to an opinion – if, but only if, you can develop fluency.

Tune into any cocktail party and you'll quickly realise that 90 per cent of those present have only a passing acquaintance with the subjects under discussion. For the most part, the conversations are overwhelmingly led by the minority 10 per cent of feet-thinkers. And as these off-the-cuff talkers circulate and gyrate from group to group, they take their volubility with them.

Picture this scene. You have been invited to a cocktail bash. A case, no doubt, of mistaken identity. Knowing nobody, you stand alone, but within hailing distance of the bar. You clutch a glass of warm wine to your bosom as though it is the last lifebelt on the Titanic and, as you gaze self-consciously around, you wish something serious would happen, like the fire alarm going off, so that you could do something sensible. Run.

Then, out of the smoky haze comes a smiling figure. He greets you. 'Hello. We were just talking about the new Covent Garden production of Wagner's Ring Cycle. Have you been?'

Now, if you are like the great majority of us, you will offer a sickly grin and say: 'No.' After all, you didn't even know Wagner *made* cycles. And even if he did, why couldn't they be called something sensible, like Rapido or Roadmaster?

Your response, then, has effectively killed the conversation. It stumbles and falls like a tranquillised elephant; and you are left to look like ignorance personified.

On the other hand, were you an off-the-cuff thinker (which you most certainly will be by the time you finish this book), you would have responded along the lines of:

'Wagner. Well, yes, I think he's possibly the most exciting/ underrated/innovative composer of all time. Loud, mind (*smile*); but certainly exciting/underrated/innovative. Did you hear the Radio 3 biography of him recently?'

Wallop! You've turned the conversation back on the questioner and you have appeared knowledgeable. Yet all you had to know was that Wagner was a composer of loud music. To such a response, the questioner is obliged either to say he did hear the programme – which is a hoot if no such programme was broadcast – or admit that he did not. Either way, you now have total control of the conversation and can take it anywhere you wish it to go.

You won by stepping outside of normal response patterns.

The temptation to reply with a simple 'yes' or 'no' spells death to imaginative thinking and creative speech.

So, where does that leave us? It suggests, as a first step, that we should compile a whole batch of innocuous responses, with which to load our magazine ready for firing. Look at it like this: a .38 Smith & Wesson beats four aces any day of the week.

When they carted Oscar Wilde off to Reading Gaol, they dressed him in the familiar arrow-covered prison suit and handcuffed him to a warder. As the pair stood in the pouring rain, Wilde remarked, 'If this is the way Queen Victoria treats her convicts, she doesn't deserve to have any.' Does this sound to you like an improvised comment, or a well-rehearsed *bon mot*?

Again, the inimitable Mark Twain on a business contemporary: 'I admire him, I frankly confess it; and when his time comes, I shall buy a piece of the rope for a keepsake.' Extempore or carefully thought out?

Yet again, the artist James McNeill Whistler was no less a conversationalist than his drinking partner Oscar Wilde. On one occasion, Whistler made a brilliant remark and Wilde admiringly said, 'I wish I had said that.' To which Whistler replied: 'You will, Oscar ... you will!'

Common sense suggests that the major portion of the famous so-called off-the-cuff remarks were very carefully rehearsed indeed. This disposes me to say that what is good enough for Twain, Whistler and Wilde, among many others, is good enough for us. Of course, at this stage in the game we are not like those mentioned above, lionised to the point where somebody is constantly standing by to record our every word for posterity. So we can afford to be less ambitious when coining phrases to be used as opening gambits to questions.

'I am very glad you asked me that,' is pretty dull, but it plays for time. As does: 'What an astonishingly good question. I hope I can do it justice.' One step up, perhaps, is, 'I am not the world's greatest authority on —, but for what it's worth I agree wholeheartedly with the sentiments of your question.'

The opening statement is a major component of the fluency aspect of responding to questions; and you should be at pains to devise a few that will sit happily upon your lips. We should now discover how to generate verbal flow in the substance of our answers.

To that end, I offer you the one-minute spiel.

The one-minute spiel

The one-minute spiel is an exercise which can be carried out at any time you are alone; while shaving or putting on make-up, driving or weeding. All you have to do is talk aloud to yourself, in a sensible, structured way on a given subject. You do this as often as your day allows, and you do it day after day spontaneously, until fluency of thought and word becomes second nature.

Sixty seconds is a long enough time when you are talking on a subject about which you have some knowledge; but it is an interminable time when you have to speak on a topic for which you previously paid little regard. But the exercise is, no question, one minute well spent. Because it is a sure-fire method of developing verbal fluency. I assure you it has worked wonders for me.

But wait. There would be no point asking you to speak on familiar themes – your wife, husband, job, hobbies – since these are things permanently at the forefront of your mind, and no truly conscious thought would be involved in your effort. You would simply slip into automatic. And that's why I am setting the topics.

Below are 20 unrelated themes. I ask you to take them in strict order and do a minute on each. If you can talk into a tape recorder, so much the better. This way, you will be able to assess your progress and hear the improvement. You will improve, of that have no doubt.

I think you will find that when you begin this exercise, you will stumble over words, um and ah, repeat yourself and experience mental blocks. This is to be expected. Most of the people on whom I've tried it at first dried up after about 20 seconds. They could go no further. With practice, however, they easily completed the 60 seconds. The object, as I've said, is to obtain a steady, unhindered flow. It's a good idea, too, if what you say actually makes sense and is logically structured, though this is not mandatory at the beginning. Later, once you've perfected flow, is the time to worry about the sagacity of it.

A few tips are in order here. Before you begin a given subject, take ten seconds to collect your thoughts. Then speak slowly – slower than your normal conversational speed, that is. Also, say whatever you wish about the subject, don't worry if your facts are wrong and your figures don't add up; let your mind explore the subject top to bottom. Unlock that right brain and *improvise*.

Here are the topics.

1. A yellow sock
2. Air travel
3. A piano
4. Beer
5. Dining out
6. Burglary
7. A red book
8. Explosives
9. Children
10. A washing machine
11. Glue
12. Psychoanalysis
13. Jam
14. Lipstick
15. Australia
16. Green issues
17. A telephone
18. Diary keeping
19. Talking for one minute
20. A good film.

Banal? Puerile? Well, possibly. Though I think you'll find it's not as easy as it seems. So do give it a whirl.

And now for a further couple of pointers. Let's take the yellow sock to illustrate them. On the face of it, you may reckon it's nigh on impossible to speak at any length on a yellow sock if you are restricted to the terms of the subject. You might feel that once you have declared that a yellow sock is a knitted garment, and is made from wool or a mixture of wool and cotton, you have explored all the possibilities and that is an end to it. On the contrary. If you run with it, improvise, think laterally, and allow your mind to probe every avenue, you will be amazed, not only at the scope of the talk, but also at what you know about yellow socks and related themes. Allow me to show you what I mean.

A yellow sock is probably yellow inside as well as outside, since the wool is dyed. This gives you the chance to swerve off at a tangent and expound on everything you can dredge up about dyes and colours. On the other hand, the sock is designed to keep the wearer's feet snug and warm – just the same as other garments, such as pullovers, jackets, overcoats, gloves; and it's a little known fact that nobody knows when or where human beings first decided to wear garments ... and so on. Again, etiquette might prompt any wearer of yellow socks also to wear a yellow tie, or a yellow handkerchief in the breast pocket. This kind of conformity to fashion is only one of dozens of fashion protocols that one comes across every so often. Like blue and green should never be seen; and wearing sneakers with a dinner jacket is just not done. And so on.

I hope you can see what I'm getting at. There are no limits to the breadth or depth of your talk. In fact, as I've said, you will be agreeably surprised at just how inventive you can be, once you dump your initial inhibitions over the side.

If we assume that you have tackled the 20 subjects and are delighted with the result, please don't run away with the idea that nothing more has to be done. Quite the opposite. You have to keep at it, and I mean keep at it. Week in and week out. For this purpose, you'll need to choose your own topics; but do so without cheating. Open any book, select any one word (a noun or pair of nouns: washing machine, shopping list) from each of the first 20 or so lines, and those are the subjects. This will narrow your opportunities to go for things that are too familiar to you.

I mentioned that your speech should be made aloud. There

is a good reason for this. If you compose the dialogue in your head, you will find yourself glossing over the stumbles; and you will unconsciously rectify errors of construction. What we are aiming to achieve, of course, is the combination of agility of thought with fluency of speech, until a truly slick delivery becomes second nature. Anyone can be voluble in the privacy of their own minds. It takes hard, unstinting work to be verbally fluent on any subject under the sun at the drop of a hat.

You take the point.

EIGHT: TALKING TO YOURSELF CAN SERIOUSLY IMPROVE YOUR VERBAL FLUENCY

However, this is only the beginning – a tough one, I'll admit, but a beginning nonetheless. Once you have mastered the one-minute spiel, you will be delighted to learn that you can move on to the three-minute and five-minute spiels.

You are joking! Who said that?

Don't give up now – you are halfway towards being one of the best feet-thinkers since Plato.

Fortunately, you can give yourself a little help with the three-minute and five-minute versions of the spiel. Here's how.

First select the subject. It will need to be somewhat more substantial than for the one-minute spiel. Give it a little thought. Then, on the back of an envelope, write five – and only five – prompters. These are to be consulted and employed during the talk. On this occasion, too, you are allowed to do a little research, via an encyclopaedia or similar reference, though you must not make the prompters longer than one line. Any other way would be tantamount to writing a script, and that's definitely not on.

The subject might be: The Loch Ness Monster. The back-of-the-envelope prompters are:

1. Loch Ness in Highlands of Scotland
2. Monster first seen AD 565 – periodically since
3. About 50 feet long. Like prehistoric plesiosaurs

4. Many expeditions launched. Photographs unclear
5. Popular myth; similar to UFOs, Bermuda Triangle, etc.

Given the scope offered by the pointers, there is every reason to be confident that the average person can talk for at least three minutes on this subject. Though knowing what you already know, I'm sure you could provide five minutes … and then some.

Look at it this way.

Prompt 1 allows you to develop your theme with a brief rundown on the Scottish Highlands. The topography, the rainfall, the tartans, the whisky – the lot.

Prompt 2 lets you air your knowledge of Britain's early history. The Saxons, Celts, King Arthur.

Prompt 3 gives you the chance to describe the monster. Your description can be as wild as you fancy, since nobody really knows what it looks like. If you know anything about dinosaurs, you are off to a flying start.

Prompt 4 puts you in a position to expound upon any scientific evidence you may have read. Surveys of the loch, underwater cameras, echo-sounding devices used to locate the monster. How do echo-sounders work?

Prompt 5 allows you to talk about popular myth and legend. Alien visitors from space, strange disappearances, ghosts, Big Foot, the Yeti.

The possibilities contained within this little lot are practically endless. But take it step by step; build gradually on what you learn. Practise the three-minute spiel for a day or two before tackling the five-minute. Time yourself accurately and hang it out until the last split-second. Before you know it, excitement will set in and you'll soon be talking for five, ten and fifteen minutes without faltering.

As you progress, your vocabulary and sentence construction will expand and improve by leaps and bounds, especially so if you take the trouble to listen to professional speakers, and make use of thesaurus and dictionary. Nobody is too old to learn a new synonym, or too erudite.

In the final analysis, you will be able to speak on any subject –

from phosphor-bronze bearings to Etruscan vases – and give the impression of having spent your entire life researching it.

When you reach this stage, no out-of-the-blue question, interrogation or accusation will faze you ever again. You will respond as if you had prepared a script. There will be no self-conscious stammering, no scrabbling around in the dark recesses of your mind for an appropriate word, no white knuckles or wet palms. And you will be looked upon by all and sundry as someone who truly knows their stuff.

You have used no crutches or lifebelts. It's all your own work.

I guess it's all about building confidence; and confidence comes only from the self-knowledge that you will never again be put into a defensive position.

Perhaps we should explore this at greater length.

Dummy runs

Just as there are only eight basic musical notes, six basic film plots and five basic motives for murder (envy, gain, sex, hatred and fear), there is a finite number of situations in which we have to stand up to be counted, that is, to make off-the-cuff responses:

1. At a business meeting
2. In a press or TV interview
3. As an apologist for something beyond our control
4. During a job interview
5. During a sales pitch
6. On the telephone.

There are probably any number of variations, but these should be enough for practical purposes. So let's devise a few hypothetical situations – really awful hypothetical situations – and see how you can acquit yourself.

1. You are at a management meeting. Suddenly, you are accused by your Managing Director of taking money from Dodgy Products Limited in return for awarding them your computer contract. The accusation, while literally untrue,

has some foundation, since you did accept a case of Scotch from that company ... which you subsequently drank.

If you admit straight out that you accepted a bribe, your job is probably on the line. If you deny it and further evidence comes to light, the same applies. How will you extricate yourself from this mess? Possibly like this:

You: 'You accuse me of taking money in return for award-ing the contract. The accusation is untrue in every respect. I don't know how I can prove my innocence, but I'm willing to present my bank statements so that you may judge for yourself whether money changed hands. I should also tell you that the contract was awarded on price and after-sales service. Dodgy Pro-ducts' quote was the best value for money of all the tenders submitted. The documentation proves this adequately.

'However, once the contract was signed and sealed, I was, as a matter of fact, offered a case of Scotch as a gesture of goodwill; and I saw no ethical reason for refusing it. If that is bribery, then it is retrospective bribery, because I was as surprised to receive it as you are, I imagine, to hear about it. I don't think there's any more to add or, indeed, any reason to pursue the matter further.'

Not bad. As a defence, it is plausible and reasonable; and it leaves room for allowing you the benefit of the doubt. You will notice that the answer addresses the main accusation head on, rejects it out of hand, presents solid, integrity-building evidence and then, and only then, touches on the whisky issue. Even so, the whisky gift is mentioned only in oblique terms. It is 'offered' with 'no reason for refusing'. There is no mention whatsoever of 'I was given' and 'I took'.

Defusing situations such as this, with the use of indirect words and phrases, is what puts the feet-thinker head and shoulders above the rest.

2. You are a prominent local councillor. Word has just

reached you that your husband/wife has been arrested by the police. As you hurriedly leave the council chambers, you see a knot of grim-faced newspaper reporters waiting to buttonhole you.

Reporter: 'What can you tell us about your husband/wife being arrested today and charged with shoplifting? Do you have anything to say?'

What I urge you not to say is that you are 'stunned' or 'devastated' by the news. As far as I'm concerned, both those words should be expunged from the dictionary. And the sooner the better. We'll give it a go:

You: 'Word of this has only just reached me. So I probably know less about it than you do. But if, indeed, my husband/wife has been accused of some offence, you may be sure that we will mount a stout defence.

  'I am going to the police station right now to find out exactly what has happened. Then I shall be consulting our lawyers. Until I have the complete facts, I can say nothing other than I am greatly concerned and take the matter very seriously. If you'll excuse me now, I shall be happy to give you a fuller statement later on today.'

Notice that you never mentioned 'arrested' and 'charged' and you certainly said nothing whatsoever about 'shoplifting'. The press will always use these words to their own ends; and in the event, should the charge be dropped or found not proven, the headlines will still remain in the mind's eye of the readers. Your husband/wife will continue to be a shoplifter in any case.

Let's do a few more; but now you're on your own. I'll set the scene, you make the responses. Length? Around 30 seconds. You may also care to switch on the cassette tape and record both the scenarios and the reply. Go.

3. As the managing director, you are hosting your company's annual dinner. A hundred and fifty employees and clients have just taken their seats. Then, the manager of the hotel

approaches you to tell you that, due to a wage dispute, his kitchen staff has walked out, along with the waiters; and there will be no banquet tonight.

You have just 30 seconds to explain the situation to the assemblage: to apologise for dragging them all there in their finery and, perhaps, to offer an alternative plan.

Away you go. Next:

4. The job interview is going well. Your qualifications are exemplary, and your experience is second-to-few in your field. The interviewer appears impressed by the whole package, and the post seems to be as good as yours. Then:

    Interviewer: 'You state in your CV that your current salary is £42,000 a year; yet your tax coding, which you seem inadvertently to have included in your application documents, indicates that you are earning considerably less. Around £30,000. Would you care to explain this discrepancy?'

Rather you than me.

5. You are trying to sell an important potential customer your firm's latest range of foolproof, undamageable computer gadgetry. This man is a legend in the business world, and everyone takes note of his opinions. If he likes your products, the word will quickly get around. So this is a crucial sale.

    For ten minutes, you have regaled him with the message that these products can be safely put into the hands of total numbskulls and will never go wrong. The customer picks up one of the products for closer examination, and as he does so, it falls to pieces in his hands!

    What you say in the next 30 seconds will determine the fate of yourself and your company.

Take it away.

6. You are alone in your married male/female boss's office. This boss is a dyed-in-the-wool authoritarian, who fires at

the drop of a paper-clip. No job is safe when his or her ire is invoked.

The phone rings and you pick it up. Without introduction, a very irate male/female voice which you don't recognise screams:

'How can you do this to me? I waited for two hours in that restaurant last night. You're using me and I've had enough! If you don't meet me in 15 minutes at Brandenburg's, I'm going to phone your wife/husband and tell him/her everything about our relationship!'

Crash! The caller slams the receiver down, and you are left with the telephone still held to your ear. At that point, the boss walks in and asks: 'Who was that?' If you explain the full gist of what you've heard, you will become a threat to his/her position. If you don't, he/she is certain to discover that it was you who withheld the caller's vital ultimatum.

Thirty seconds should be enough to get you off the hook.

While we're on the subject of telephone responses, there are a couple of ploys used by the feet-thinker which you should know about. These are essentially stratagems for gaining time while you frame a response or produce what is being requested.

A customer telephones you asking for a firm delivery date on a sale previously negotiated. This aspect of the deal has slipped your mind and you have forgotten to make arrangements with the despatch department. Given a couple of minutes' breathing space, you could rectify matters. So:

'Yes, I have the date, Mr Boat, but unfortunately I'm not in my own office. I'll go through right away and then call you back. About five minutes should do it.'

Or:

'My secretary has all the documentation on her desk, Miss Fitt. If you'll give me a minute to check, I'll give you the firm date. Can you hold, or shall I call you back straight away?'

Or in really dire circumstances, where the despatch department has closed for the night:

'You've caught me in one of our late-night meetings, Mrs de Point. I've fixed a firm date, of course, but I don't have it with me. I assume you'll be leaving the office quite soon; so, if I may, I'll call you first thing in the morning. Is that OK?'

Since the caller has no idea of the actual situation, he or she must take you at face value. Some might say that such ploys are less than honest. On the other hand, you are ultimately interested only in maintaining good customer relations. And that's worth all the little white lies in the book.

In closing this chapter, I urge you to spend as much time as possible practising and rehearsing the various spiels. The more you practise, the easier it will become, and the more fluent will be your conversation. If it's of any consequence, I do one-minute spiels in the shower each morning, and on such mind-enhancing subjects as plumbing, the working principles of soap, and the theory of why the towel is always out of reach from the cubicle.

And if I have to do it, so do you.

CHAPTER
6

Creative thinking leads to inspirational speaking

'Don't just stand there, say something.'

Anon

In this chapter, we shall be talking about words; and about the delivery of words. It's no secret that I have a passion for words. This love affair is unrequited, as usual, but I pursue it with an enthusiasm that would levitate tables.

Of course, words are my business; and I don't expect anyone to be as obsessive about them as I am. Even so, if you have any ambitions for becoming a feet-thinker, you would be well advised to have more than a passing acquaintanceship with words. Because it is with words, and words alone, that we express our thoughts; and the better we are at expressing those thoughts, the more creative we become. Creativity, after all, is what separates man from animal. Human beings paint, write, act and sculpt seemingly for the hell of it, since very few can actually make a living from it. As a matter of fact, they do creative things for reasons considerably more important than mere fun or distraction; they do them for personal satisfaction, for the warm glow of ego, and for the approbation they receive from their fellow man.

Translate that to the business world, and the creative sales-people, inventive lawyers, ingenious computer programmers are not only applauded for their skills, but rewarded for them in hard cash. They have that spark of talent which puts them ahead of the field.

In the advertising business, there is an adage which runs: complex problems have simple, easy-to-understand *wrong* answers. Now and again, however, the right answer dawns like a veil being lifted. I say 'now and again'. In fact, the process has to be constant, otherwise the people concerned will shortly be looking around for less demanding occupations.

After three decades of devising advertising campaigns for some of the world's best-known products, I still have no clear perception of where the right answers come from. But they come, and they come, remarkably enough, at exactly the right time. At the last minute.

Picture the scene. A copywriter and a designer are shut away in order to come up with a handful of brilliant concepts which may help to sell somebody's reciprocating sockets. They read the marketing brief, without enthusiasm. For the following hour, they talk about everything and anything but the problem in hand. Conversation ebbs; the copywriter gazes idly out of the window; the designer makes paper aircraft and sends them floating around the room.

Then, as if at a signal, both begin to scribble on pads. 'What about so-and-so?' offers the designer. 'Yes,' replies the copy-writer, 'but what if we were to take it further to such-and-such?' This dialogue may continue for several hours or several min-utes, but the spark has been struck. Very soon the tinder will ignite and the campaign concept will burst into flame.

So why didn't they do this right from the start? How come they wasted so much time? Simply, the prevarication and the daydreaming is all part of the creative process. It acts to dull the influence of the left brain, and waken the right.

If I had a pound for every time I have been witness to the

above scenario, I should not be larking around like this giving writers a bad name. I should be sailing my yacht in the Bahamas, giving sailors a bad name. Yet, this is how it happens. What has this got to do with thinking on your feet? Everything.

It so happens that the best copywriters and designers can often come up with acceptable ideas in minutes rather than hours, and in seconds rather than minutes. They are the ultimate feet-thinkers. Followed pretty closely, of course, by people like salespeople, lawyers and doctors.

Nobody expects a structural engineer or an insurance actuary to give you an answer to a problem on the spot; but if your doctor fails to diagnose what is wrong with you before you leave the surgery, you will be excused for thinking he is not a very good doctor.

Now, if you were in a lifeboat with a doctor, a structural engineer and an actuary, and one of these had to be thrown over the side in order to keep the boat afloat, I wouldn't mind betting that your first choice of victim would be the actuary. So, as he goes floating off into the distance, you suddenly realise that he is the only one with sufficient maths to navigate you towards somewhere solid – like land.

Which leaves us to suppose that certain people are expected to be feet-thinkers and others aren't. But had the actuary been a feet-thinker, he would have made his abilities clear, and more likely than not it would be *you* who was about to shake hands with Davy Jones.

So, ask yourself these questions. If people expect me to think on my feet, am I giving them what they want? If they don't expect it, why don't they? And if the answers embrace any reason other than that you are an insurance actuary, my advice is to keep reading. (With apologies to those of you who happen to be insurance actuaries.)

Creativity in speech doesn't mean using impossibly long words and ridiculously convoluted sentences. Creativity in speech means using ordinary, everyday words, but in such a way that the audience believes the words are being used for the first time.

Listen to an old pal of mine, Joe Baker by name, in full flight about advertising research:

'I have never been much in favour of any research of any kind. I resent the expense of it, the inaccuracy of it, the pseudo-holiness of it and the arrogance of it. This attitude causes me to be pooh-poohed by the world's pooh-poohers. You can't argue with figures, they say. Well, if you can't argue with figures, what in God's name can you argue with?

'The interpretation of statistics depends wholly and solely upon the point of view of the person evaluating them. For this very reason, they are open to reasonable doubt by anyone who has an IQ greater than the average flannel. And let me say this. Anyone who spends his life evaluating statistics should put two and two together and figure out that he is on a hiding to nothing.'

I love it. Delivered in a tone of authority, it leaves the opposition bewildered. And there's not a highbrow word or phrase anywhere in sight. Joe Baker is now in the Great Debating Society in the Sky, but this gem lives on.

We're supposed to be talking words – let's do just that.

As a copywriter, I am aware of a list of the most persuasive words in the language; and I use them with impunity. They are:

You

The most influential word you'll ever speak, both to an audience and to an individual. Equally, an individual's name is the most important noun ever devised. Use it, and use it often.

Free

Gaining something for nothing is the desire of everyone on the planet. Also, *freedom*, as in freedom from drudgery, problems, and so on, is equally emotive.

Simple

Once you realise that the human race is fundamentally lazy, this word offers acknowledgement of, and acquiescence with, their laziness.

New

Think of the rush to buy the new-letter registered cars every August, plus the kudos gained from owning the vehicle, and the value of 'new' is obvious.

Discover

'It takes just a minute to discover how useful this product will be.' How often have you been persuaded to buy when presented with such a statement? The word brings out the explorer in all of us.

Guaranteed

If it's guaranteed, they have nothing to lose if they go along with your proposition. Similarly, 'no-risk' and 'proven' give the impression that all the wrinkles have been ironed out.

Results

A very powerful word, indeed, once you qualify it by spelling out the *benefit* of the results to the listener.

Safe

This implies no risk, and therefore projects a sense of security. Like 'reliable', the word carries overtones of dependability.

Save

Everyone likes the notion of saving: saving time, saving money, saving worry.

NINE: USE EMOTIVE WORDS

Latch on to the power of simple words. Appeal to the emotions by employing words that will promise some kind of benefit to the listener – and if it's an ego benefit, so much the better. 'I love you' is arguably the most powerful phrase in the language. 'You are correct in every respect' runs it a close second.

I have deliberately left out the words 'quality' and 'value'. These are tired old words which, in their usage, have become virtually meaningless. Used on their own, as they often are, with nothing to back the claim, both are singularly bereft of any conviction. Therefore, unless you qualify them by explaining how much value or what kind of quality, please don't use them. To point this up further, I ask you to think about the phrases 'quality time' and 'value-added' which are used throughout the land by people who apparently give no thought to what they are saying. Do they mean anything to you? Likewise me.

As I always say, if you have something worth saying, you can't beat words for saying it. But these must be good words, emotive words, power words. In normal conversation, many of us intersperse our dialogue with words and phrases that serve no real purpose. They are there as a kind of padding, to upholster our message. And when they are used on a regular basis, they become irritating.

'This is it', spoken in agreement to another's statement, is a classic example. 'As it were' is another. 'Apropos of nothing' and 'At this point in time' are others.

Clichés of this kind are fine if they are used to augment a message, but upholstery for its own sake detracts, confounds and annoys.

Also, it is a good idea to stay away from long and obscure words. Even among the intelligentsia, top-drawer words are often misused. So to employ a blue-chip word that might be confusing to the listener or, worse, to use it wrongly, does more damage than if you were to address your audience in words of one syllable.

In any case, there is no mistaking the meaning of an everyday word. And egos are undamaged by them.

Conversely, I am all in favour of words that target the emotions (like those given above), and even more in favour of using metaphor and analogy to beef up your speaking style. Just so long as those metaphors and analogies are original. There can be no worse opening to a speech than to address a formally dressed audience with: 'I feel like a thorn between all you roses.' It's not only old-hat, it's embarrassing. But to say something like: 'Am I in the right place? This looks like an audition for *The Magnificent Ambersons*,' should make everyone feel pleased to be there.

If you were to say to an audience: 'I suppose you're wondering why I've asked you all here?' you might get a titter. On the other hand, you'll get a full-blown laugh with: 'I see we have a full house. Who were you expecting ... exactly?'

In my travels around the country, speaking to a wide variety of audiences, I have concluded that people can spot a 'robot' speaker, someone who is merely going through the motions, a mile away. But they warm, oh, how they warm, to enthusiasm. When you believe in what you are telling them, when you say what you mean and mean what you say, you have them in the palm of your hand. And when you can spice those sincere beliefs with powerful words and phrases, the world is your oyster.

For what it's worth, I always kick off my advertising seminars with the line: 'I reckon that much of today's advertising is like a man who winks at a girl in the dark. He knows what he's doing ... but nobody else does.' This opener has the effect of demonstrating exactly where I stand, and promises startling revelations. It's simple, it's straight to the point, and it's controversial. I should probably pack up at that point, since it doesn't get any better. However, I'm sure you follow my drift.

Obviously, phrasing plays a great part in the delivery of a line. But the pauses are just as important. The ellipsis (the three dots – nobody expects a non-editor to know the word) in the above opener shows where the pause, a long pause, comes. The great Frankie Howerd could milk a pause for all it was worth. Indeed, he got bigger laughs from pauses than from punch-lines. But the value of pacing your words and leaving enough space between the phrases, to allow them to sink in, cannot be overstated.

The rule of three

I suppose one could, if the money was right, produce an entire book on phrasing and pauses alone. But for us, right now, there is one style of phrasing which must be mentioned. It is the rule of three. Meaning three phrases which make sense individually but which, in combination, reinforce the issue and magnify it out of all proportion to its real worth. The rule of three operates like this:

'It is good for the country.
It is good for the people.
And it is good for the individual.'

Once again, politicians are adept at the rule of three; and there is one in particular who uses it every time he speaks in public. When employed correctly, the rule has a hypnotic rhythm which practically forces you to listen, and leaves you pretty much convinced when you have. In any event, it is a superb tool for less articulate types like you and me. What's more, it can be employed in just about every circumstance.

For instance: 'This product is powerful; this product is easy to use; and this product is cost-effective.'

Or: 'I will give you the answer; I will give you the answer in simple terms; and I will give you the answer now.'

The object of speaking is to be heard and understood. With this statement of the patently obvious, there is very little value in using words and phrases that are of dubious meaning, tortuous and inflated or so clichéd that the listener's hackles rise at the very sound of them. To help you obtain a clearer insight about this, I include the following hackneyed or obscure words and phrases, and provide alternatives more acceptable to the ear.

I don't say for a moment that these words and phrases should never be used under any circumstances. My feeling is, however, that the less they are spoken, the better off we shall all be.

Aside from that, it is always a good idea to speak in the active sense rather than in the passive. The passive voice is for communiqués by EC commissioners and should be avoided, along with EC commissioners themselves, like the plague.

'The latest statistics on the life-cycle of the ice-cream cone can be purchased from ...' That's passive. 'Buy the latest statistics on the life-cycle of the ice-cream cone from ...' That's active. Simply by thinking of the person you are speaking to, rather than the item you are promoting, the case changes. Thus: 'Initially, a wide range of material will be issued to students,' is so passive it's almost asleep. To change it to the active, first identify the students, then what they will be getting. 'Students (or, even better, you) will receive a wide range of material at the start.'

To get into the active habit, concentrate on starting sentences by naming the person or organisation to whom, or about whom, you are speaking: you are ... we can ... Bob and Jane recommend ... Polymer Plastics accepts...

Which is all well and good. But why are some people better able to use words than others? Or, more properly, since they use only normal, everyday words, how come they are so agile with them?

Well, some read, read, read, everything in sight; and they also have the gift, unlike many of us, for remembering what they read. Then they recycle it to anyone who will listen. Others play mind-games with themselves.

Clichés, circumlocutions and hoary old chestnuts

At this juncture At the present time At this point in time Even as I speak As of this date	Now Right now
At some later moment At some future date At some future point	Later
At that moment in time At that time At that point in time	Then
Subsequent to	After
At which time During the time that On the occasion of	When During

The question as to whether Whether or not	} Whether
Owing to the fact that Due to the fact that On account of the fact that	} Since Because
Come to a decision as to Reach a conclusion as to	} Decide
Make mention of	} Mention
After very careful consideration	} Having considered
On the grounds that As a direct result of On account of the fact that By virtue of the fact that Owing to the fact that	} Because
Be cognizant of Fully sensible of Completely *au fait* with	} Know
He is a man who She is someone who	} He She
Despite the fact that	} Although
With reference to In regard to Pertaining to	} About
At an early date At a future moment	} Soon
Exhibit a tendency to Evince a predilection for	} Tend
Come into contact with	} Meet
In close proximity to At close quarters with	} Near

During the time that	While
It is often the case that	Often
Had sight of	Saw
Came into the hands of Was in receipt of	Got
Is of the opinion that	Believes
Scheduled for discontinuance	To be deleted
Bottom line	Final analysis
Conceptualise	Think over
Crisis situation	Crisis
Initiate	Begin
Infrastructure	Facilities
Impact negatively	Worsen
Inoperative	Out of action
Interface	Meet
Methodology	Rules
Modality	Style
Networking	Connecting
Normalise	Stabilise
Optimise	Make most of
Parameters	Limits

Prioritise	}	Set in order of importance
Shortfall	}	Deficit
Systematise	}	Organise
Time frame	}	Schedule
Upwardly mobile	}	Successful

Mind games

Mind games have the effect of getting those little grey cells activated, much the same as paper-aircraft manufacture and daydreaming did for the designer and copywriter earlier.

Some while ago, I invented (or, at least, I think I invented) a game which can be dragooned into service at practically any time. It works like this. You think of a town, any town, and then devise a pub name appropriate to it. If that isn't as clear as it should be, allow me to demonstrate.

For instance, there could be the Centipede at Crawley, the Highwayman at Andover, or the Whole Loaf at Nuneaton. Not to mention the Four Flusher at Deal, or the Pen at Wigan – which I will explain to my non-journalistic, non-metropolitan friends if they have the strength to ask.

Well, are you already punting around in your mind for suitable offerings? This game is, I tell you, as addictive as salted peanuts. Once you start, it will take an insidious hold on you, and you'll find yourself poring over the gazetteer at every available moment. As things go inexorably from bad to worse, you'll get more sophisticated. Twisted titles will start forming in your mind whether you like it or not. The Two Cubes at Dyce. The Disco at Rockingham. The Son at Leamington Spa. And so on.

The effect of all this inventiveness, I have found, is beneficial in every respect. It clears the creative decks and opens the mind.

There are, I know, dozens of different mind games. You might, perhaps, try devising your own Spoonerisms. At the bery vest they'll stop you becoming ned from the deck up. I have backed my rain to devise some examples, but I think I will sever nettle to it. Oh, here's one: 'Where is the Slack Bea?' To which you might reply, 'Is that as the flow cries?' I'd better stop flaying the pool, eh?

Daft, it may be. Nonetheless, it will help drag inspiration out of those dark, uncharted depths.

Openers and end moves

Research has shown that the average TV-watcher has an attention span of around three minutes. It's also pretty well-known that people remember the beginnings of programmes and the endings – the bit in the middle tends to be forgotten very swiftly.

Knowing this, we realise that when we address an audience, any audience, our first words and our last words should contain everything the listener needs to know. The middle part can be reinforcement or mere padding.

Barristers, whose clients' freedom lies in the balance of their words, are well trained in the art of placing important messages at the start and end of addresses.

'My client is honest; he's a family man, a charity-worker and an animal lover, members of the jury ... He is good to his mother and, as I will prove, ladies and gentlemen, has clearly been fitted-up by the police.'

If you try to remember these two sentences in five minutes' time, I suggest the words 'honest', 'members of the jury', 'good to his mother', and 'fitted-up by the police' will most easily come to mind.

A last word on words from Ugo Betti:

'Thought itself needs words. It runs on them like a long wire. And if it loses the habit of words, little by little it becomes shapeless, sombre.'

What did I tell you?

CHAPTER 7

It must be fun

'Pleasant words are the food of love.'

Ovid

Whenever the late Magnus Pike appeared on television, his audiences always numbered millions. They tuned in deliberately to watch this learned, if a little whacky, scientist. Another great television presenter is Patrick Moore; and wherever he appears, he is applauded to the rafters.

Care to know why Messrs Pike and Moore made it so high in the popularity stakes? Because of their enthusiasm. No, I'll rephrase that, it's because of their passion.

If you remember, Magnus Pike could barely contain himself while a question was being put to him. Then, when he came to speak, the words tumbled out in a torrent; his arms waved, his lips smiled. He was so engrossed in making his point that little short of an earthquake would have silenced him.

Here's the point. You may be as erudite as Messrs Pike or Moore, but your delivery will make or break your presentation. You may be the best in your field at what you do. Fine. Yet, if you don't see your task as a mission to persuade, if you are afraid to let your enthusiasm show, if you lack passion, then your ideas will not gain the currency they deserve.

So the next time you are invited to make a point, at a party, as the best man at a wedding, in a job interview, to the board of directors, or as a spokesperson on radio, jump right on it and make it swing!

TEN: WORDS WITHOUT ENTHUSIASM RING WITH ALL THE CONVICTION OF A BELL WITH NO CLAPPER!

It's no secret that, as the rest of us, audiences like to be liked. There are a couple of speakers I know who treat their audiences, if not with disdain, then certainly with arrogance. And they wonder why they aren't as successful as others. They talk down; they sound to the audience as though they have done all this before; and they brook no argument against their precepts.

You will have heard of the Agatha Christie play *The Mousetrap*, the longest-running play London has ever seen. Over the years, actors have come and gone, though many played the same part for years. As a member of the audience, you would never have known that the people on stage had delivered the same lines and performed the same actions, night after night, week after week, month after month.

And that's the trick with regular speaking. Every occasion should seem to the audience like the very first time.

Meeting your audience

What about the audience? How do you establish a rapport with them? Where you are familiar to them, as in a company management meeting, you will know in advance who is a disciple and who isn't. In which case, deliver your presentation, with plenty of eye contact, to those who respect your ideas. Then leave it to the partisans to convince the begrudgers after the event. Never, ever aim a presentation directly at people who may dislike you personally, with the purpose of trying to win them over; their reactions to your words will put you off your stride, and you'll be seen to ignore the good guys. Even if your detractors stay mute, you will be able to see their dislike in their body language; which may be enough to throw you right off course.

Where you have to make a full-blown speech, it pays to remember that the 200-strong audience is actually made up of individuals. There are 200 egos sitting there waiting to be massaged. Thus, you won't be very far into a talk before you recognise the individuals who are buying your act. They'll nod as you make your points; folded arms will drop on to laps; and now and again, a brief smile will flicker across their faces.

Once you identify them, work on them. Use plenty of eye contact with them, more, in fact, than you do with the stone-faced characters around them; and make a point of directing a comment, here and there, straight at them. And smile when you do so.

What happens with this little trick is that other members of the audience can see that you have struck up a relationship with the buyers – and they too will want a piece of the action. Psychologically, they are telling themselves that if the woman in the red dress likes you, why shouldn't they?

When you are well into your speaking stride, you can take things a step farther. Ask the nearest buyer a simple question about the gist of what you're saying. Make it an aside, rather than a confrontational gambit; but be sure everyone can hear it. Say 'Does that make sense?' or 'Am I getting this across ok?' The reply is sure to be a nod or a smile, or both. Now you are buddies, and the rest of the audience will want to get in on the act. Buyers will start popping up in all quarters. You've got them in the palm of your hand.

Handling questions

Some speakers make it clear at the outset that they will take questions from the floor at any time; and I'm one of them. Others like to save question time until the end. Either way, the secret is to stay in control.

Some well-meaning books on public speaking insist that questions should be left to last. They then go on to tell us that we will be given questions which we cannot answer, and when this happens, we should be honest and admit it. Further, they say we can ignore the difficult ones. How you do that exactly, I don't know and they don't enlighten. But try that on a Glasgow audience and they might just allow you to live.

My feeling about it is this. If you have the nerve to set yourself up as an authority on a given subject, you ought to know that subject inside out and backwards. Excusing yourself on the grounds, say, of technology going ahead so fast that you have not caught up with a specific piece of information, is to sell your audience short.

No, sir and madam. Either answer the question direct or, if you are unsure of your ground, use the flannel techniques learned in earlier chapters.

There is one other way of dealing with a difficult question, turn it back on the audience. Say 'That's a tricky one. I wonder if *anyone else* here knows the answer.' The implications behind the use of the phrase 'anyone else' – meaning that you do know the answer – will not be lost on you. Anyway, while they are deciding whether or not they do, you have earned enough breathing space to compose a decent reply.

I happen to enjoy question time at seminars because it allows me to engage in conversation with the audience. Which is another reason why I invite questions at any time. A speech is formal, while questions are, by their nature, informal. So if a few questions come early on in a talk, it helps to break the ice. Since the dialogue is no longer one-sided, it brings the audience closer. We are now on talking terms, which in turn helps me to relax.

Other ways of breaking the ice are to ask a question or two collectively of the audience. For instance, if you are talking on the subject of merchant shipping, you might ask for a show of hands on how many people read *Lloyd's List*. Or if it's marketing, ask whether they are familiar with the law of diminishing returns. Or whatever.

Under no circumstances – and I will repeat that – under no circumstances ever pick on someone and ask them a direct question, unless, via previous dialogue, you have a damn good idea that they can answer it. I'll tell you why. If they cannot answer, they will look and feel stupid. The audience will probably giggle a little, but they will experience intense embarrassment for the unfortunate questionee. And you may be sure that they will reserve the right to warm to you. And another thing: quite a number of them will be wondering whether they are next.

Business presentations, of course, are somewhat different from the formally delivered speech. Questions generally arise as the pitch progresses. Such a circumstance can throw many otherwise excellent presenters. The answer is to be so well prepared that, whatever the interruption, you can weather it, then pick up the thread as easily as you left it.

I can't speak for many other industries, but I know that presenters in advertising agencies rehearse their pitch in-house before making the formal presentation to a client. During this rehearsal, not only is the framework of the pitch and order of speakers ironed out, but also a scenario of the potential questions and disputes is developed.

Clearly, pre-emption is better than fudge.

Eliciting questions

Now let me pose you a question. What do you do if, after you've delivered what you believe is an interesting talk, nobody in the audience has a question for you? Believe me, it happens. Often, people are afraid to speak out. Less often – I'd say rarely – you may have covered everything worth covering in your talk.

Well, it seems obvious that your audience is not as warm as you may have hoped. So here's what you say: 'One of the questions I'm often asked is ...' Then you can chat for a minute and hope someone will soon feel comfortable enough to put a question to you. Another workable line is, 'I noticed a few puzzled frowns when I was talking about so-and-so. Was it as clear to everyone as it should be?' Whereupon you restate that particular case. Both these lines will keep you in control of the situation and let you down gently if no questions are forthcoming.

We discovered how to deal with argumentative questioners of all kinds earlier on. But how do you tackle hecklers?

First, I think you've got to understand *why* you have a heckler on your tail. Generally, a heckler believes he knows more about the subject than you do. If you suspect this is the case, politely invite the little devil to come up and finish your talk. In the normal course of events, that should shut him up. He may even be bold enough to take up your offer; but I am willing to lay odds that he will soon discover that the audience doesn't want him. Collapse of stout party.

The other kind of heckler is the one who is simply out to cause disruption. The thing to do is ignore him in the first instance but, if he persists, present him with the short, sharp and pithy put-down you have prepared for such an eventuality.

Professional speakers have their own favourite put-downs. Mine, passed on to me by one of the speaking greats, runs as follows.

Heckler: 'You're talking a load of old codswallop.'
Speaker: 'Thank you, sir. Where are you from?'
Heckler: 'Me? I'm from Birmingham. What's it got to do with you?'
Speaker: 'Well, sir, there is a bus leaving for Birmingham in five minutes ... Be *under* it!'

I've never yet had to use it, which is odd, bearing in mind the standard of my material. There is, of course, no accounting for taste.

Know your lines

A few pages back, I spoke about ad agencies doing rehearsals. Just how word perfect should a feet-thinker be? Anyone who hopes to make others sit up and take notice, I believe, should know his subject so intimately that he can recite it in his sleep. The salesperson must have product knowledge right down to the last nut and bolt. The marketing manager must be so familiar with the needs and make-up of his target audience that he can practically call each of them by name. The public speaker or after-dinner speaker must be as word and gesture perfect as any good stage actor – which is approximately what he is.

How is this achieved? I'm sorry to say it again, but there's no alternative: it's practice.

I deliver the same talk on the same subject, month after month. Yet I never deliver exactly the same talk twice. Occasionally, I am asked to do an hour; at another venue, they want a full day. This means that concepts have to be tailored and precepts edited.

Therefore, I write each script from scratch. This is not as difficult as it sounds, because the subject remains the same, only the duration alters. And when I have the script timed for length, I record it. The cassette then goes everywhere I go, and I play it until I am sick of it. As browned off with the sound of my own voice as I may very well be, I now know the lines word for word. Sure, I also prepare prompter cards, which I don't hesitate to use on the day. Nevertheless, I am so familiar with it that I can afford to abuse it. I can stop to take questions, or wait for any other interruption to subside; and I can pick up where I left off without a falter.

In the early days, before I found the method that was right for me, I made every mistake it was possible to make. I lost my place, showed certain slides before they were due, and became generally flustered. Then I went along to see Francis Albert Sinatra perform at the Albert Hall. What he did was a revelation.

At one point in the concert, when he was halfway through a song, a woman rushed down the aisle clutching a bottle of Jack Daniels. Sinatra, being the man he is, stopped singing, leant down to take the bottle and planted a kiss on the woman's cheek. Meanwhile, the orchestra is 16 bars ahead. Did he join them? Did he hell! No – he continued from exactly where he had left off. How the band lost 16 bars, in the blink of an eye, to pick him up is one of life's great mysteries. But this is precisely what they did.

What I learned was that the true professional is so well rehearsed that he can never lose sight of his theme.

Now, there will be those who will disagree vehemently with all of this. They will say that memorising a script will stultify delivery and force the speaker along a too narrow path. I say nonsense. If you have the whole spiel in your head, you are in a better position than ever to ad lib to the occasion, or tell a pertinent joke, or take a question. Even accept a bottle of Jack Daniels and plant a kiss, if necessary. Delivered properly, your script doesn't have to sound rehearsed. And you never have to say 'Where am I?'

Yet thinking on your feet is no big deal. As long as you are sincere. As long as you are enthusiastic. As long as you know your business. As long as you are well rehearsed.

So we've come to the point where you are approaching the end of your speech or presentation. If you've taken questions throughout, there's no need to hang it out any longer than necessary. Do you want to go out with a bang or a whimper?

I once delivered a talk to a large throng of librarians. I won't go into why they felt it necessary to listen to me; suffice to say that the session was due to last for an hour. It seems that I spoke with such enthusiasm, that they allowed me to go on for 90 minutes. Librarians are, by nature, nice. Anyway, noticing the time, I stopped in mid-flow and simply said, 'If you have been, thanks for listening,' and started to walk off. Several voices murmured in surprise and someone asked, 'Why have you stopped?' This was followed by a stream of applause the strength of which I had never received before, nor have I since.

Like the man said: always leave them wanting more.

Were I you, I'd now make me come up with some solid ideas for closing a presentation or a speech, bearing in mind that the close is as important as the opening – and probably more so, on the grounds that it is almost certainly the one bit your audience will remember.

Oh, very well, then. Here are five off-the-cuff ways to close with style, with dignity and with your self-respect nicely intact.

Winding up

1. The standard summary

Recap briefly on your major propositions. Add a new, juicy fact (one which you have deliberately held back), then make a statement that congratulates your audience. Something along the lines of: 'It's been a long time since I met a group of people who were so keen to know more about this subject. I thank you ... most sincerely.'

2. The rhetorical question

For this example, let's say you are talking advertising to a group of business people. To close, restate one major point from the main talk, then ask a question to which agreement is the only answer. Maybe this way: 'I said earlier that it doesn't matter how much money you put behind a bad idea, it will always remain a bad idea. After tonight, you won't be having any bad ideas – will you?'

3. The call to action

At the end of a business presentation, when all the facts and figures have been put to the client, it greatly helps to present him and his team with a gee-up. We'll assume that the gist of the presentation is to persuade the client to buy a financing package or install a new computer system. 'On the basis of what we've seen, I think you ought to do it. Indeed, I think that you think you ought to do it. Ladies and gentlemen – why don't we do it?'

4. The apt epigram

You have delivered a proposal to your boss which could completely change the way your company operates in a certain field. He or she appears ambivalent. So try an appropriate quotation. 'One doesn't discover new lands without consenting to lose sight of the shore for a very long time.'

5. The ego massage

You are selling to a tough prospect. 'I believe in this product, Mr Boat. I wouldn't be here if that wasn't the case. And, since you are someone I respect, I shouldn't be taking your time if I didn't know that you will benefit from it.'

Stage fright

The Guinness Book of Records contains a startling fact about speaking in public. It says, in essence, that man's number one fear is that of making a verbal presentation to a group of people. This fear is greater than the fear of water, greater than the fear of fire, greater, even, than the fear of death.

Frankly, I am not in the least surprised. With the possible exception of going flying with me, there can be no more stressful a situation. Nervousness is nature's way of telling us that we have bitten off more than we can chew. Never mind. The greatest achievers in this world always, without fail, bite off more than they can chew. This is the basic difference between the dreamer and the go-getter; the amateur and the professional. The amateur does something only when he feels like it. The professional, on the other hand, does something when he doesn't feel like it.

Controlling stress is an art in itself. Here are a few of the methods I use, if not to kill the butterflies, then at least to make them fly in formation.

Think positively

Don't ever tell yourself that you are going to fail, because, as sure as the sun will rise tomorrow, you will fail. When fear raises its head, take yourself firmly in hand and say, 'I know this subject possibly better than anyone. The people I am about to address want to learn something from me. I shall knock their socks off.'

Breathe

This may come as a huge surprise to you, but breathing is the mainstay of your existence. The more air you take in, the more oxygen circulates within the bloodstream, and the more nourished is the brain.

So sit down in a quiet room. Place your hands in your lap and breath in deeply to a slow count of seven. Hold it momentarily, then breath out again to a slow count of seven. Do this three times. I think you will be delighted at just how relaxed you will feel.

Dynamic tension

Stand upright. Clench your toes as tightly as possible to the count of five. Relax.

Now clench your toes and calf muscles to the same count. Relax.

Now clench your toes, calves and thighs to the count of five. Continue this clenching and relaxing with every area of your body: include stomach, chest, shoulders, lower arms and upper arms in sequence.

It takes a while to complete, and it has much the same effect as banging your head against a wall. It's lovely when you stop. The feeling of utter calmness that invades your body has to be experienced to be believed. What happens, I think, is that you translate the anticipated stress of speaking to the here and now.

It's a fact that, having given a talk, no matter how good or bad you were, you experience relief on finishing that borders on euphoria. Thus, by doing the muscle-tensing exercise, you get the relief and the euphoria before the event. Therefore, the rest is easy.

There must be a clinical psychologist somewhere who has done work in this area, and who can explain it. Until we hear from him, you'll have to make do with my explanation.

Check out the venue

Some venues come as a huge surprise. They turn out to be bigger or smaller than you imagined. They echo; they are so configured that the slide projector is at one end of the room, while you will be at the other; and they have windows so architectured as to accurately throw the blinding rays of the morning sun directly into your eyes.

If you can do it, therefore, always view a venue in advance

and ask for blinds, extra lights or a microphone to be installed well before the day.

Be prepared

You know your script. You are intimately familiar with the agenda, but do you know that the overhead projector blew a bulb the day previously? Are you aware that because somebody else packed up your gear on the last outing, 50 per cent of the slides in your carousel are upside down? You'd better be.

Don't booze

Perhaps I should temper that. If you are a dedicated drinker, as I am, a half-pint of beer or a small Scotch will do you no harm whatsoever. In fact, it may just have the desired effect of helping you to relax. Under no circumstances, however, should you sink more than several, because even confirmed drunks don't like to see drunkenness demonstrated in others. Why? I can't imagine. But they don't. There is an appropriate time for booze. After the event. Cheers!

I now propose to move from the general to the specific. Are you coming?

CHAPTER
8

Shape up to the media

'Editor: a person employed by a newspaper, whose business it is to separate the wheat from the chaff, and to see to it that the chaff is printed.'

Elbert Hubbard

When the media take an interest in you and want to interview you, you'd better be ready for 'em.

As the spokesman, probably the reluctant spokesman, for a company that has allegedly put a number of smaller companies out of business, you will be in for a tough grilling. As the promoter of a new product, or scheme, you will be quizzed as to its worthiness. As someone who has written a controversial book, watch out, the press is about. As an expert on a particular subject, you may be called upon to speculate on the outcome of a recent event, or predict the likelihood of its recurrence.

Either way, you're under the spotlight of publicity; and you, and only you, can make it a favourable one for yourself. You may find that the following pointers are worth noting.

Magazines and newspapers

If a reporter telephones asking for an interview, lose no time at all in securing a copy of the magazine or paper in question.

Clarify its readership profile, and carefully note its editorial style. From this, you will make your own mind up about whether you wish to continue with the appointment.

You should be aware that journalists are trained to pry into other people's business. They may promise on their word of honour that some unguarded remark you have made will be treated as off the record. But don't be surprised if you see that remark, generously embroidered, in colourful black and white. Reporters also know how to read between the lines, and the really good ones miss absolutely nothing. Trying to buy insurance by pouring drink into them simply doesn't work. On the one hand, journalists are notorious boozers and can sink a barful without breaking sweat. On the other, being bought puts their job firmly on the line. So forget it.

If you are frank with a journalist, the chances are that he or she can be turned into an ally. Where you are open and helpful, they will come to rely upon you as an expert/authority, and will contact you when they need good copy. This process is reciprocal. When you have something to say, you'll receive a ready ear.

All in all, say nothing that you don't want to see in print. It's that simple.

Radio

When the telephone rings and someone at the other end of the line says they are calling from Radio Neasden and wants to conduct a live interview with you now, this is the moment of truth. This is when you find out, once and for all, whether you are a feet-thinker.

You will be broadcasting live; so every word, every gasp, every stutter, will go immediately into the homes and cars of thousands of indifferent people.

There is a good side to this, however. The station called you for a reason – you may have published a book, or won substantial work promotion. In which case, you will already know about it and can therefore be prepared.

The in-studio, recorded interview is somewhat different. In

fact, it's a lot different. You may be answering questions for a solid half-hour, yet, when the interview is aired, you find that you have been cut to three minutes. Worse, it's plain that only the minor points of your message have been used. The major ones are on the floor of the editing suite.

Therefore, when you're in the studio, make your major points at the very outset of the interview; then make them again at the close. In this fashion, you create double the chance of having them aired.

Television

As with radio, ten minutes in front of a TV camera can be edited to just a few seconds. So the same advice applies: get your message in fast.

Never look directly into the camera, always keep your eyes firmly on the interviewer. Don't twitch, fidget or scratch. The tiniest movement, which people would never normally notice face to face, is vastly exaggerated when it's duplicated on that little screen.

Additionally, wear sober clothing: grey, blue, green, brown, beige and, at a push, pale yellow. Bright reds seldom reproduce well. You may care to think twice about wearing lots of jewellery; this gives the impression of flamboyance and even flaunted wealth. It also jangles. Bold colours and flashing gems tend to distract the viewer's attention from your message.

CHAPTER 9

Watch your body language

'A man's behaviour is the index of the man, and his discourse is the index of his understanding.'

Ali Ibn-Abi-Talib

One of the greatest entertainers in the world is Frank Sinatra. He not only has a voice of quality, and intonation and phrasing of real creativity, he also has that indefinable quality called charisma.

When he walks onto a stage, even when it is crammed with musicians and stage-hands, he is the only person there. How come? He isn't tall and muscular and therefore able to stand out. He isn't stunningly handsome. And attired, as he usually is, in black dinner jacket, he's no differently dressed from the tuxedo'd musicians who surround him.

Can I tell you what I think makes him stand out? It's studied presentation. And it comes about through practice. The walk, the smile, the hand gesture, the shrug. I reckon he rehearses these with the same dedication as he rehearses his melodies.

Don't you think it would benefit us if we took a few leaves out of his book? Me, too. In the first instance, we'll examine the three most important aspects of body language.

Eye contact

Watch Sinatra's eyes when he moves on to a stage. They embrace everybody in the room – not just once, but several times. Immediate eye-contact with members of your audience offers both a greeting and a signal that you are happy to be there.

Posture

A slummocky posture tells everyone that you are uncomfortable with your lot. You demonstrate a lack of confidence. You are trying to make yourself as small as possible, just like the hedgehog who rolls himself up in order to present the worst possible target for predators.

Clearly, you don't want to be there.

Therefore, stand tall. Place your feet 12 to 14 inches apart, and push those shoulders back. If this posture seems unreal at first, then practise it in front of a mirror. The improvement will be obvious and quickly achieved.

And when you move, say from centre stage to projector, move slowly, and keep your eyes on the audience. Never turn your back on them; they don't do it to you. Think how miffed you would be if they did.

Voice

You don't need to possess the old BBC standard received accent to be able to communicate to an audience. Indeed, many people would rather listen to a brogue or a burr.

What you must have, though, is clarity of speech. This means a delivery which is both slow enough to follow, and words that are enunciated clearly enough to understand.

Gabblers abound in every walk of life, as do mumblers, glottal stoppers and effers for tee-aitches – if you're still with me. If your mode of speech is hard to follow, how can you expect them to understand your ideas?

The only way I know of improving your speech (and I have one of the worst combinations of London/Dublin/USA/Scots accents you might care to imagine) is to read aloud to a tape recorder. You won't like what you hear, no one does. Yet what you hear can almost certainly be improved upon by taking pains to pace delivery and pronounce the words more clearly.

Finally, when people are frightened, their voices tend to rise in pitch. This is a dead giveaway to any audience. Make a point, then, of pitching your voice lower than normal if you are in any way nervous. It will eventually recover of its own accord; and nobody will know the difference.

Which takes us on to the generalities of body language. I won't do much more than list the body actions and suggest what signals these actions transmit. This is because I am no authority on the subject, merely a pipeline. Were I to go further, I should only end up by making myself look foolish. And I do that too often as it is.

Good manners and body language

You will, I am sure, devise your own put-downs if you are seriously in the business of becoming a feet-thinker.

However, all audiences appreciate good manners. When addressing people, employ the good old 'sir' and 'ma'am' (to rhyme with spam). Never say just 'yes' to someone who has a hand raised to ask a question. It's arrogant and off-putting, it demeans the person in question and it won't endear you to anybody. Sometimes, you may be able to elicit a name or two from audience members. Once you have them, remember them and use them.

I suppose it goes without saying that picking nails, digging fingers into ears and scratching armpits and heads, or worse, is taboo. You laugh? Make no mistake about it, there is nothing worse than being captive to a picker or a digger, nor anything more calculated to turn an audience off. And that means any audience, from your pub cronies, to a sales presentation, to a thousand-delegate seminar at the Royal Festival Hall.

I hate to bring this up, but do you dress to please yourself or to please others? I only ask because a well-dressed presenter gains at least five points out of ten for general appearance. Being at least as well turned out as your audience is something that is expected of you. You are the guv'nor, after all. Being better turned out is a bonus.

There's a bit more to it than that. When you look good, you feel good. And if you feel good, you can evoke the buzz far more easily.

Signals

Hail fellow well met. The signs of honesty and cooperation

- Palms presented (open-handedly)
- Tilted head
- Coat undone
- Tie loosened
- Sitting on chair edge, upper body leaning forward, knees slightly apart, hands on knees
- Wrists exposed (in women).

Help! Nervousness and insecurity

- Bad or no eye contact
- Hands in pockets
- Arms folded across chest
- Fingernail picking or biting
- Ear tugging
- Brushing non-existent lint from clothes
- Preening hair
- Jingling keys or money in pocket
- Fidgeting.

Don't like the look of you, chum! Distrust

- Rubbing nose

- Arm barrier – arms folded or one arm crossing chest in the fashion of Napoleon
- Rubbing eyes
- Scratching back of neck.

It's great to be here! Confidence

- Hands behind back
- Fingers steepled
- Hands clutching lapels
- Sitting well down in a chair, feet apart
- Both hands behind neck
- Open palm gestures.

Is it time to go yet? Frustration

- Tongue clicking
- Finger stabbing and pointing
- Hand gestures palm down
- Hand dragged through hair
- Massaging neck
- Fists tightly clenched.

Am I buying your act? Reflection

- Eyes peering over glasses
- Stroking chin
- Cradling chin
- Cleaning glasses
- Head tilted
- Eyes narrowed.

This is by no means the definitive work on body language. To find out more, lay your hands on a good book on the subject. What the above sets out to do, though, is demonstrate that there is as much to body language as meets the eye – if you care to look.

Sometimes, a person can be saying one thing with his mouth, and his body can be projecting something else entirely. It cannot be a bad idea to know when this is happening ... to others and to you.

As a feet-thinker, you can use body language very much to your own advantage. For your part, you can project a positive image; and on the part of your listeners, you can observe how well you are going down, and tailor your presentation accordingly.

Powerful body language supports your message and compels the listeners to go along with you. Ask Frank Sinatra.

One final, but rather important point. Audiences, whether they are made up of three people, or three hundred, generally want you to succeed. More often than not, they are *willing* you to succeed.

You can use this phenomenon to worthwhile effect by projecting body language which assures them that you are worth rooting for.

Above all, and whatever happens, smile.

Conclusion

Thinking on your feet means being able to take charge of any situation at any time. People who can do this are not as rare as you might suppose. The average police officer, for instance, takes command of a whole variety of weird situations every day of the week. The same applies to salespeople and business people generally.

You can probably name two people within your sphere of things who have similar academic backgrounds and do identical jobs, yet one is far better thought of by his peers than the other. We might try to explain this on superficial grounds by saying that person A is far better looking than person B and therefore commands more attention. All right, looks can certainly sway opinions, but not for ever. Personality is always the key factor. You can prove it simply enough by looking at those who have made it big in the entertainments industry. I'm pretty certain that the most abidingly popular of them – those who last – are only averagely good-looking; and a few are downright plain.

Like I say, it's personality that sways opinions, and personality is a derivative of inner confidence. And where does inner confidence come from? From knowing your subject inside out and backwards.

Feet-thinkers know that you can't sell soap-powder until you sell people on the idea of having clean clothes. Feet-thinkers see beyond the traditional limits of verbal intercourse and strive to achieve new dimensions. The wind that fills the sails of the feet-thinker is the same wind that sinks the boats of those who tremble at the thought of setting sail.

The sheer nerve it takes to stand in the spotlight of general opinion can be summed up in the words of Rene Anselmo, who spent 30 years building a communications empire and at the age of 63 gambled everything to launch a television satellite. 'If everybody tells you it can't be done, you're on to a good thing. But that also means you're on your own.'

As a feet-thinker, you automatically label yourself as different. When you succeed, others will label you special. What's wrong with that?

So feet-thinking, when all is said and done, is a state of mind. And good feet-thinkers know that developing an agile brain and a persuasive tongue is the road to fortune. They are also aware that gentle seduction beats aggressive assault any day. If only on the premiss that it allows you to go back for a second go at a willing 'victim'. Consequently, feet-thinkers reap the benefits.

I hope this book has been as much fun for you as it has for me. I also hope it achieves what it sets out to do.

And if you have been, thanks for reading.

Further reading from Kogan Page

Andrew J Bradbury (1995) *Successful Presentation Skills*
Daly, Pete (1991) *Talk Small! A Guide to Effective Small Talk*
Decker, Bert (1989) *How to Communicate Effectively*
Denny, Richard (1994) *Speak for Yourself: Tested Techniques for Improving Your Presentation*
Haynes, Marion E (1988) *Effective Meeting Skills*
Hurst, Bernice (1991) *The Handbook of Communication Skills*
Mandel, Steve (revised 1993) *Effective Presentation Skills*
Peel, Malcolm (1995) *Improving Your Communication Skills, second edition*